Contents

Acknowledgements v

Prefatory Note vii

Chapter 1- The St. John's Program: The Beginning of
its Conception 1

Chapter 2- Virginia, Chicago, and the Opportunity at
St. John's 13

Chapter 3- The New Program at St. John's 27

Chapter 4- Public Interest and Internal Changes Under Barr
and Buchanan 39

Chapter 5- Criticism from Outside and Inside and Effect of
World War II 53

Chapter 6- The Fight with the Navy in Wartime and the
Departure of Barr and Buchanan 67

Chapter 7- Kieffer's Presidency and the Beginning of Weigle's 89

Chapter 8- Jacob Klein, Dean 101

Chapter 9- A Time of Stabilization and Deeper
Understanding 113

Appendix 127

Notes 130

Acknowledgements

This history of what was known as the "new program" when it was instituted at St. John's College forty-six years ago this autumn has been in process for a number of years. Originally undertaken more than a decade ago by Stringfellow Barr, it was never completed because of Mr. Barr's failing health. About five years ago J. Winfree Smith of the faculty agreed to take over the project. The history here presented is primarily the result of Mr. Smith's patient and dedicated efforts.

The research, writing, and publishing of this important work, however, could not have been completed without the interest and generosity of a number of individuals and organizations: Carol U. Berstein, Eulah C. Laukes, Paul Mellon, Eugene V. Thaw, The Isle of Wight Fund, the Joseph H. Hazen Foundation, the Ford Foundation, the J. M. Kaplan Fund, and the Fund for Tomorrow. The college is indebted to these loyal supporters.

Thanks go also to Thomas Parran, Jr., of the college staff for editorial assistance and production supervision on the project.

But very special appreciation goes to Mr. Smith for telling so eloquently the story of how the college's present unique liberal arts program came into being.

Edwin J. Delattre
President

Annapolis
Summer, 1983

Prefatory Note

It has been several years since it was first proposed that there be a history of the institution of the St. John's program. Stringfellow Barr intended to write such a history, but found that, as he grew old and his memory failed, he was unable to do so. John Kieffer then undertook the task, but was prevented by serious illness from carrying it out. After his death, the proposal was in abeyance until one evening at Santa Fe Mr. Robert Bart, then dean of the Santa Fe campus, and his mother urged me to write the story. I said I would consider it. Mr. Bart then made the suggestion to President Richard Weigle, and at his request I consented.

At the time it was thought by some that it would be preferable to have someone from outside the college tell the story on the ground that I might be partial to the curriculum and to the men who had most to do with starting and establishing it. It is true that I owe an immeasurable debt to Barr and Buchanan, who were my teachers at the University of Virginia in the 1930s, and also to Klein, from whom I learned much, especially during my first years as a member of the St. John's faculty. I can only say that I have tried in this narrative to stick to the facts and to make no inferences or judgements not warranted by the facts.

The narrative covers only about twenty-one years in the life of St. John's College, the years in which the program was started and became established. It does not pretend to describe in any detail improvements in the curriculum since 1958, especially in the teaching of modern natural science. Nor does it begin to cover the years of Richard Weigle's presidency and his contribution to the college.

I should like to express my thanks to several persons who have been of help in the enterprise: to Miss Charlotte Fletcher and Mrs. Kathryn Kinzer, St. John's librarians, for allowing me the use of a room in the college library; to Miss Miriam Strange, registrar for many years and later archivist at St. John's, for helping me locate relevant documents and for giving me the benefit of her extensive memory; to Mr. Mortimer Adler for allowing me the use of his files relating to St. John's; to Mr. Thomas Parran, Jr., St. John's publications director, for his meticulous care in preparing the work for publication; and to Mr. Leo Radista for reading the manuscript and making valuable suggestions for its improvement. Finally, I should like to thank those who contributed the funds that made it possible for me to have the leisure to devote to the work, and whose generosity is acknowledged within these pages by President Edwin Delattre.

J. Winfree Smith

St. John's College
Summer, 1983

CHAPTER 1

The St. John's Program: The Beginning of its Conception

There was instituted at St. John's College in Annapolis, Maryland, in 1937 a curriculum which has ever since made St. John's different from other colleges in America and from the undergraduate departments of American universities. This curriculum is now followed not only in Annapolis, but also on a second campus of the same college in Santa Fe, New Mexico, where students entered for the first time in 1964. It is the intention of this work to tell the story of the origin and formation of the curriculum and the story of the college during the years that the curriculum was being established. But first it will be necessary to describe the curriculum.

It is based on the assumption that it is possible to formulate a whole plan for undergraduate education. Therefore, there are, with minor exceptions, no elective courses. The student is expected to study everything that is taught, those few things excepted. Likewise, the faculty are expected to teach everything that is taught. Since usually their study before coming to St. John's has been specialized, they have to make any earlier special interests subordinate to working within the whole program of the college. They have little time for special research or for writing. They see their principal task as teaching, teaching through learning in conversation with their students and with their colleagues.

Another assumption on which the curriculum is based is that part of education consists in reading, and that, on the whole, it is better to read books of superlative worth by the best thinkers and about central questions than second- or third-rate books by lesser thinkers. It is also assumed that it is possible within limits to say what these books are, to make a list of them. The curriculum, then, is based on the reading of "great books", not "*the* great books", since they do not constitute a fixed canon; of the some 119 authors in the first St. John's list published in 1937 less than half remained in the 1980 list, though in many cases there had now been introduced different books by the same authors. Also, books by other authors have been added. It has been understood from the beginning that the list is always subject

to revision and that the inclusion or exclusion of a given book has to be defended with good reasons. Naturally, some books have always been included, and presumably always would be, as for example the Bible and works of Homer, Plato, Aristotle, Euclid, Augustine, Thomas Aquinas, Dante, Copernicus, Machiavelli, Descartes, Newton, Kant, Hegel, Nietzsche, and Einstein, to name a fair sample.

From these examples one can see that it is wrong to speak of the St. John's curriculum as a neo-classical revival if by that one means that its ordering principle is a return to Greek and Roman classics. If, however, one means by a classic a book or an essay, whether ancient or modern, or a scientific experiment that is of the utmost excellence in its kind, then the curriculum is based on the classics. But then Einstein's 1905 paper on special relativity or Rutherford's experiment (as performed by Geiger and Marsden) on the scattering of alpha-particles is as much a classic as Plato's *Republic* or Virgil's *Aeneid*. There is no presumption that ancient thought (which includes the thought of Democritus and that of Sextus Empiricus, as well as that of Plato and Aristotle) is necessarily superior to modern thought or that medieval thought is superior to modern thought or, on the other hand, that truth is necessarily the daughter of time and hence that modern thought must be superior to that of antiquity or the Middle Ages.

The books don't teach themselves. They have to be read. Reading makes extremely varied demands upon the reader. Poetry makes a kind of demand that prose works do not. Plato's dialogues make a different kind of demand from that of Aristotle's *Physics* or Kant's *Critique of Pure Reason,* and all of those make a different kind of demand from that of Newton's *Principia,* for the reading of which a study of Euclid and Apollonius is essential; or from that of Einstein's 1905 account of special relativity, for which a study of partial differentials is prerequisite; or from that of Minkowski's 1908 paper that geometrizes Einstein's special relativity, and for which a study of Apollonius is necessary. There are, therefore, at St. John's classes called tutorials in which languages and mathematics are studied. When the curriculum was introduced in 1937 (and to a large extent it is so still), these tutorials were thought of as fostering investigation of and practice in the traditional liberal arts; the linguistic arts of the trivium—grammar, rhetoric, and logic; and the mathematical arts of the quadrivium—arithmetic, geometry, astronomy, and harmonics. The arts of the trivium are encountered in the learning and translating of Greek and French texts as well as in the close study of certain English texts. The attention is directed to the ways in which language embodies grammatical, rhetorical, and logical elements and forms and the ways in which all contribute to the intelligibility of a text. The liberal arts of the quadrivium can be distinguished from one another as far as ancient mathematics is concerned, even if the distinctions cannot be maintained in modern mathematics (What is a point in projective geometry? A triple of

numbers?). In any case, the St. John's mathematics tutorial explores these differences along with the question of what mathematical things are and to what extent the knowledge of them brings a knowledge of the world in which we live. Astronomy and mathematical physics find a place in the mathematics tutorial.

The books have to be read. A careful and thoughtful reader (even one with little formal schooling) will constantly ask questions of what he reads. To some he will get an answer from his reading. There may be others that he will ask that lead nowhere and still others that it will not occur to him to ask. Hence, another assumption of St. John's is that a college is different from a library, that one learns by listening to talk about what one reads and by talking about it. One might, for instance, after having become thoroughly confused in an effort to read Kant's critiques, come to understand them as a consequence of listening to intelligent and informative lectures. But the St. John's mode of education rests on the further belief that one learns more through listening and talking in a well-ordered conversation than through merely listening. The Platonic dialogue suggests a model for such conversation. Only instead of a Socrates, or an Eleatic or Athenian stranger, and one, two, three, or a few more participants, there are two faculty members and about twenty students in each of the seminar groups into which students of all years are divided to discuss assignments in the great books. One of the two faculty will start the discussion by asking a question related to the reading. Then a student will respond with his opinion as to what the text means to say about that question, or as to what he thinks the truth of the matter is. Another student may then question his opinion or state his own. Thus a conversation develops, often, but not always, in the form of a contest between opposing opinions. There are only a few rules governing it. One is that one must say what is relevant to the question or the subject under discussion. Another is that, whether one is a faculty member or student, one must be willing to support with reasons whatever one says. Any student can ask the question, "Why do you say that?" In many institutions teachers who do not allow what they say to be questioned by the students get away with nonsense. Although almost everything in the way of material for study is prescribed for St. John's students, they have a large freedom in the sense that within the very wide bounds of what is prescribed they are not only allowed, but encouraged, to question everything. Questioning what is within the bounds often leads to questioning the bounds.

It is these two things, the belief that one can learn through a certain kind of coherent conversation and the willingness to question everything, that lead people to say that there is a Platonic or Socratic presence at St. John's.[1] There is no such presence if one means by such a presence the dominance of Platonic teachings, which, of course, is not to say that there are no Platonic teachings or that they are not worth discovery and careful

attention. What St. John's College means to be engaged in is radical inquiry. This means a readiness to pursue Socrates' questions, but equal readiness to question the presuppositions of Socrates' questions, to ask, for example, with Nietzsche, "Why the will to truth?" And to ask, in turn, about the presupposition behind Nietzsche's question.

The reading and discussion of books is for the sake of learning. What is to be learned, of course, is not just something in a book. It is not as if there were, on the one hand, the book, and on the other hand, the "real world" with no connection between. The books read at St. John's are about things that belong to the common experience of all human beings, the sky above us, the earth our home, the many things above us and around us, human life on the earth in all its sameness and diversity. They ask questions and make statements about these things. It is not always apparent to the student that the questions a book raises must become his questions if he reflects upon the things around him, upon himself, and upon the things above. This means that it is the special task of the teacher to help the student see that questions that may have seemed unreal questions are real questions, and are his questions. The seminar particularly is the locus for this at St. John's.

In the junior and senior years the seminars are suspended for eight weeks and the members of the two classes participate in what are called preceptorials. The preceptorials provide an opportunity for students in those two years to study intensively a particular book or a particular subject which they choose from a list of books or subjects offered by their seminar leaders or other faculty members. There might, for instance, be a group of from five to eight students, including both juniors and seniors, reading Wittgenstein with one of their teachers.

In addition to the language and mathematics tutorials, the seminars, and the preceptorials there is the laboratory. Since 1937 there has been the constant endeavor to make modern natural science an integral part of the curriculum. Much of the teaching of modern natural science occurs in the mathematics tutorial where the endeavor has been quite successful. It has been less successful in the laboratory where there has been at times a tendency to present biology, chemistry, and physics as separate studies in a conventional manner. The experiments performed or witnessed by the students usually have not been devised by them, but have been repetitions of experiments crucial to great scientific discoveries made in the past. In connection with these experiments the students read several original papers by Dalton, Faraday, Driesch, Mendel, Einstein, Bohr, and Schrodinger, to name only a few.

There is, finally, in the sophomore year a music tutorial where one learns about the seven-tone scale and the twelve-tone scale, about melody and harmony, about keys and modulation. There certain great classics of music

such as Bach's *St. Matthew Passion* and Mozart's *Don Giovanni* are analyzed in detail. These works are also discussed in music seminars where frequently the center of the discussion is the question how the music sound sequence fits the drama and the words and contributes to the whole that one not only hears with one's ears but grasps with one's intellect, or grasps with one's intellect through hearing with one's ears. In spite of what is agreed upon in practice, there is still some question as to what the music of the music tutorials is as a liberal art.

Most Americans think of education as a preparation for something else. Some think of it as a preparation for a job or career which will enable one to earn money for the comforts and conveniences, as well as the necessities, of life. Others with a larger vision think of it as a preparation for the intelligent exercise of one's responsibility as a citizen and perhaps as one called to public service. It should be clear from the description given that St. John's does not seek to prepare its students for the bourgeois life. Nor is its primary goal the making of good citizens or political leaders, though it might be hoped that the proper study of books that have to do with the good that is public and common would contribute to the formation of political wisdom and political virtue. St. John's does not believe that education is one thing and life another, that life begins when education ceases. Though there is no illusory expectation that all of its graduates will all their lives be thinking about all of the same questions that occupied their discourse during their college years, there is the assumption that knowledge is good for its own sake and, if knowledge is not attained, that the understanding and the improvement of opinion that are obtained in the thirst and quest for knowledge are also good; and there is the hope that the habit of reflective inquiry that has been formed in the college years and that results in such understanding and improvement will continue with benefit to the soul and to society that is greater than any comfort or convenience of life.

The St. John's program came to be as a result of the vision, courage, and initiative of two men especially, Stringfellow Barr and Scott Buchanan. Also, there were quite unusual circumstances that made it possible for them to do what they did. It is conceivable that there should be other colleges like St. John's, and indeed there are other colleges which resemble St. John's in some respects, and in some colleges and universities programs that resemble the St. John's program. But one cannot forget that the St. John's program would hardly have come into being but for those exceptional men and the exceptional circumstances.

The exceptional circumstances can be briefly stated. St. John's College in the spring of 1937 was in woeful condition. The Board of Visitors and Governors had, just before the stock market crash of 1929, become feverishly engaged in investing in real estate, i.e., in the purchase of certain properties, mostly colonial mansions like the exquisite Hammond-Harwood House

Stringfellow Barr and Scott Buchanan.

and the exquisite Brice House. They had done so with the expectation that Francis P. Garvan of New York would finance a restoration of colonial Annapolis under the auspices of St. John's as John D. Rockefeller, Jr., had financed the restoration of colonial Williamsburg. Mr. Garvan lost heavily in the crash and was unable to furnish the financial backing the college needed for its project — in any case, a strange project for a liberal arts college to be involved in. The property of the college had been mortgaged. There was no money to pay the interest on the mortgage and not enough to meet operating expenses. The college had had three presidents in ten years. The last of the three, Amos W. W. Woodcock, had been asked to resign principally because he vetoed a decision of the faculty and granted a degree to a student who had failed to meet the requirements for the degree, which action caused the Middle States Association of Colleges and Secondary Schools to revoke the accreditation of the college. As a consequence of all these things, the board were ready to give Barr and Buchanan *carte blanche* to make drastic changes at St. John's.

Barr always said that the St. John's program originated with Buchanan.[2] That is true. Barr himself, however, was quick to grasp much of what Buchanan was after, became enamored of it, and had a remarkable ability to present it vividly and dramatically to the public. What emerged in 1937 as the St. John's program had been forming in Buchanan's thoughts since his own undergraduate days at Amherst. He got his B.A. there in 1916 and continued for a year as an instructor in Greek. Alexander Meiklejohn was then president of Amherst. Meiklejohn discouraged lecturing and encouraged teaching and learning by discussion. He considered it the president's role to question both faculty and students about what they were doing and why. He loved to be invited to the student's informal discussions, where he persistently questioned them and got them to question one another. Buchanan was to say shortly before his death, "It was through Alec Meiklejohn that the whole living Socratic method became clear."[3]

In 1919 Buchanan went as a Rhodes scholar to Balliol College, Oxford. There he read Plato's *Republic* with A. D. Lindsay and later Kant's three critiques. He already had an interest in Kant because of Meiklejohn's own special devotion to the author of the "critical philosophy." It was at Oxford that he met Stringfellow Barr, who was a Rhodes scholar at Balliol at the same time. In "Scott Buchanan, Teacher" Barr describes his initial fascination with Buchanan, his subsequent and temporary dislike of what seemed to be truculence and trickery that ended in making fools of people, and the resumption of their friendship which lasted until Buchanan's death in 1968.[4] He certainly thought that Buchanan as a Rhodes scholar still in his twenties was a Socrates to him, he being also a Rhodes scholar still in his twenties.

Returning to the United States in 1921, Buchanan enrolled as a graduate student in philosophy at Harvard. As a graduate student he was already

a rebel. He and six of his fellow students issued a manifesto to the Harvard philosophy faculty, demanding, among other things, two faculty leaders for a seminar.[5] At Harvard he found particularly valuable his study of mathematical logic which came to play a part in his doctoral thesis, later published under the title *Possibility*. That thesis set forth a general methodology for relating all possible philosophies. Buchanan claimed that it was Alfred North Whitehead who saved it from being rejected by the philosophy faculty. There are two stories about the thesis. One that he himself has told is that the faculty showed it to Whitehead after remarking that they couldn't understand it and that Whitehead, upon reading it, replied, "If you can't understand it, so much the worse for you." The story as told by Whitehead's daughter to Bernard Peebles is that upon their saying, "It's nonsense," Whitehead had answered, "Yes, but it's the right kind of nonsense." John Dewey, reviewing this same thesis when it appeared in book form, wrote of it, "a first class piece of work" that "offers seeds with which to sow many a flourishing intellectual garden."

Buchanan, after finishing at Harvard in 1924, went to New York, where for one year he was an instructor in philosphy at the College of the City of New York, and then became assistant director of the People's Institute at Cooper Union. Always critical, as Meiklejohn had been, of conventional education and especially of conventional departments of philosophy, he welcomed the task of planning lectures at the People's Institute for adults who were not working for credit or degrees, and who paid only twenty-five cents to attend a lecture. The lectures were designed to bring together immigrants from the lower East Side of Manhattan and "intellectuals" from the upper West Side. The former were "first and second generation immigrants whose migration to this country had uprooted them from intellectual and educational traditions which they feared they would lose in America."[6] The latter were "internal migrants, remnants of native American intellectual and philosophic movements." They were not a typical group of American adults. Their previous backgrounds had made them especially responsive to what the People's Institute offered. They were eager to learn and to understand. They subjected the lecturers to sharp questioning. Some of them formed a club to continue discussion after the lectures. They met in what had been an artist's studio on Twenty-second Street. Each time there would be talk about the lecture but also informal discussion of a book, such as Dante's *Divine Comedy* or Eddington's *The Nature of the Physical World*. Another group was formed to discuss Plato's Dialogues. Buchanan was at the center of both these groups.

There were two things he found missing in the minds of these students at the People's Institute. One was poetry and the other mathematics. He consequently announced that he would give a series of lectures on "Poetry and Mathematics" and spent the following summer preparing to do so. The

notes for the lectures eventually resulted in a book by the same title; the title itself indicates that Buchanan was trying to see as interrelated what many people might think of as entirely separate and unconnected worlds of thought and imagination. The content of the book shows that he had begun to make the acquaintance of the mathematical and mathematico-physical classics of Descartes, Galileo, and Newton and had touched upon projective geometry. This was an important episode in the formation of what resulted in the plan for the St. John's curriculum.

It was the delivery of these lectures and the Writing of *Poetry and Mathematics* that led Buchanan to the notion of the traditional liberal arts as presenting the necessary formal structure for learning. Richard McKeon, who was then at Columbia University and who had begun to lecture and lead discussions for the People's Institute, had recently returned from Paris where under Etienne Gilson he had studied medieval philosophy and medieval education. McKeon insisted, as Buchanan reports, that "I had stumbled upon a rediscovery of the seven liberal arts, the trivium—grammar, rhetoric and logic—and the quadrivium—arithmetic, geometry, music, and astronomy." He further insisted that "we three [Mortimer Adler was the third] ought to proceed with a revision of the traditional forms and reconstruction of them for the sake of the order and articulation they could bring to the contemporary college and university."[7] The three had many conversations among themselves about the liberal arts and proceeded to lecture on them. They were not out to revive them exactly as they had been understood or practiced in the Middle Ages or as they had ever been understood or practiced. They were "using the forms of the original European universities and filling them with the content of modern learning."[8]

One could from several sources compile a list of great books that Buchanan had read by this time. It seems that it was from Philip N. Youtz, whom he had called in to organize small study groups at the People's Institute, and also from Mortimer Adler that he got the idea of using great books, discussed in seminar fashion, as a means for liberating the soul from prejudices and ill-conceived opinions. Ever since the Renaissance, people had at various times drawn up lists of great books.[9] Thomas Jefferson drew up a list of books for the education of his nephew, Peter Carr, which includes books by Homer, Sophocles, Euripides, Herodotus, Thucydides, Plato (Socratic dialogues), Virgil, Shakespeare, Milton, Swift.[10] He considered Bacon, Newton, and Locke, because of their books, "the three greatest men the world had ever produced,"[11] and in order that the students at the university he was founding should have correct political opinions, he got the Board of Visitors to pass a resolution setting forth the view that the texts to be used in political studies should be Locke's *Essay on Civil Government,* Sidney's *Discourses on Government, The Declaration of Independence,* the *Federalist* (presumably also the Constitution, since the *Federalist* is an exposition and

defense of the United States Constitution), the resolutions of the Virginia Assembly in 1799 on the alien and sedition laws, and Washington's Farewell address.[12] Jefferson's great books are a sizeable fraction of the St. John's list. It has sometimes been said that the St. John's program is a return to the kind of education that formed the thought and character of the founding fathers of the American republic.[13] Indeed, from the list given and from Jefferson's statement, "In all cases I prefer original authors to compilers,"[14] we might suppose that there is something in it. Yet it becomes clear that Jefferson himself was held captive to the prejudices of modernity and was far from seeing that ancient authors have serious questions to pose to modern authors. In a letter to John Adams, he writes, "We must dismiss the Platonists and Plotinists, the Stagyrites and Gamalielites [presumably those who sat at the feet of Gamaliel], the Eleatics and Gnostics and Scholastics, their essences and emanations, their Logos and Demiurgos, Aeons and Daemons, male and female with a long train of Etc., Etc., Etc. or shall I say at once Nonsense,"[15] Plato, Aristotle, Parmenides, St. Paul, Thomas Aquinas, and many others are all thus summarily dismissed with a semblance of humor. A mere list of great books does not tell us much about any plan of education in which they are to play a role, if nothing is known about the principles guiding their choice, how they are going to be read, and the ends their study serves.

In any case, Buchanan was accustomed to refer to only two lists antecendent to the St. John's list, (1) a list prepared by Sir John Lubbock for the Workers and Mechanics Institute in England published in the Daily Telegraph for August 2, 1895, and (2) a list introduced for the general honors course at Columbia in 1920 by John Erskine with the strong support of Nicholas Murray Butler, then president of Columbia. Erskine had attempted in 1917 to inaugurate at Columbia an honors course based on reading great books, but had failed because of faculty oppostion. At the end of World War I Erskine was associated with the American Expeditionary Force University at Beaune in Burgundy, a university for doughboys overseas. There still persists a story that some of these doughboys had seminars on great books, but Erskine himself wrote to Scott Buchanan on December 27, 1938, "As far as my memory serves me, we had no selected reading list at Beaune," and in the catalogue for the Beaune University there is no reference to such a list or to any course based on such a list. Lubbock's list, which had about a hundred entries, included forty-nine that have never been on the St. John's list. There were forty-six books originally written in English as opposed to eighteen in the present St. John's list. The most notable differences, however, are that Lubbock's list included eight eastern works (among them the *Koran,* the *Analects of Confucius,* and the *Ramayana* and *Mahabharata*) and no mathematical or scientific works with the exception of two by Darwin, whereas the present St. John's list includes no eastern works, unless one

considers the Bible an eastern work, and sixty-two mathematical and scientific works if one counts among them essays and papers such as the Einstein paper already mentioned. Erskine listed authors rather than books. His list of fifty-two authors contains thirteen who wrote in English, no eastern authors, not many authors of mathematical and scientific books (though the names of Galileo, Newton, Lyell, Darwin, and Pasteur appear), and there are other significant additions to Lubbock's list, such as Thomas Aquinas, Kant, Hegel, Marx, Nietzsche, Tolstoy, and Dostoevsky.

Seminars on great books were already a going thing at Columbia when Buchanan went to New York in 1924. Erskine was still there, but Mortimer Adler and Mark Van Doren were by then more deeply involved than Erskine. They soon became close friends of Buchanan's and later established an intimate and lasting relationship with St. John's College. One of the great events of this period was Buchanan's discovery of Thomas Aquinas. Adler in his autobiography describes the excitement with which he, Buchanan, and Arthur Rubin, a long-time friend of Adler's, began to read Thomas Aquinas.[16] Buchanan, not long before his death, said of this experience that "for the first time in my life I knew what the Christian doctrine was. [As a youngster he had been quite a churchgoer in the Congregational Church in Vermont and at Amherst had been a rather unusual secretary of the Christian Association.] I was terribly impressed and felt very deeply involved, with a deep belief in the Christian doctrine. In some way I think that's still true with me." At the same time he could say, "I suppose I'm more Greek than anything else."[17] About a decade after he first encountered Thomas Aquinas and when he had joined the philosophy faculty at the University of Virginia, he had got as far in the *Summa Theologiae* as the treatise on the sacraments which he was reading with intense interest and which inspired several lectures in which he sought to relate the seven sacraments to everything under the sun. One of these lectures on "The Sacraments and Mathematics" he expected Robert Hutchins and Mortimer Adler to tear to pieces.

CHAPTER 2

Virginia, Chicago, and the Opportunity at St. John's

The story of the origin of the St. John's program and the story of Scott Buchanan's intellectual adventures during the twenties and thirties of this century are of a piece. We shall, therefore, have to consider more of what he did and said up to September of 1937 when the program became a reality at St. John's.

In the fall of 1929 he left New York to join the philosophy faculty at the University of Virginia. He soon found life there depressing. On October 17 he wrote to Adler, "We are just beginning the second lap of what is an old course, and it feels like wholesale disillusionment. Faculty, students, landscape, accent, housekeeping, even leisure, all are flat and unprofitable."[1] The pattern of the old course was, unhappily, to be repeated several times in Buchanan's life. Nevertheless, he was able to report that he was looking forward to reading Hegel's *Science of Logic* and a few days later that he was engaged in that.

The exchange of correspondence between Adler and Buchanan during the nineteen-thirties shows that they and Richard McKeon had become a close trio, and that the three of them thought of themselves as engaged together in a common enterprise, which might simply involve sharing what Adler called their "little game with philosophy" or it might involve attempting to make radical changes in American higher education. Even before Adler went to Chicago,[2] Buchanan was urging upon him that Virginia was a better place than Chicago for their operation and that he was going to suggest to Albert Balz, then chairman of the philosophy department at Virginia, that he invite Adler and McKeon to join the department. He stated his opinion that the three of them had laid down the fundamental points in methodology which they were showing signs of applying to subject matters that would give rise to diversity and independence among them. "I should like," he wrote, invoking and considerably changing the Socratic image, "to have you and Dick nearby to play midwife and nurse to my monsters to see that they are exposed before it is too late — and I should especially enjoy returning the service."

In 1930 Adler went to Chicago to assist Robert Hutchins in establishing a new curriculum there based on the reading of great books. He, however, wrote to Buchanan shortly thereafter that he was not primarily interested in the reorganization of the University. "I am intersted, first of all, " he said, "in the little game with philosophy that you and I like to play, and to that end I am terribly interested in having you and Dick here . . . But you certainly couldn't expect Bob to enjoy our little game." At that time Buchanan had only begun to know Hutchins and to renew the friendship that he had formed at Oxford with Stringfellow Barr. The latter had begun teaching history at the University of Virginia in 1924 and had acquired a well-deserved reputation among the students for his witty and brilliant lectures in modern European history. Barr had a healthy respect for what the historian has to do to get at the facts, but he also thought that the historian can never ignore the question of the meaning of the facts. He himself at that time was a follower of Spengler and interpreted history as a sequence of relatively unconnected culture-civilizations each one of which, like an individual human being with unique characteristics, is born, grows, reaches its acme, falls into decay, and dies. He saw the culture-civilization of the West as being in decline.

During Buchanan's years at Virginia he and Adler continued to write to each other, and the questions of what they might do in education and where they might do it kept recurring. Buchanan, while teaching philosophy , was pursuing his own education, particularly in mathematics, physics, and logic. He was working on projective geometry with John Jennings Luck, an excellent mathematician with a large stomach and fondly know among Virginia students as "Pot" Luck. Carroll Sparrow, an interesting, witty, and versatile physicist, began giving a course in modern physical concepts chiefly for Buchanan's benefit. Buchanan was also reading Appollonius' *Conics* in Heath's abbreviated edition from which he expected to learn more about "the relevance of proportions in projective geometry and the problem of duality." Still depressed with life at the University of Virginia, he was being more and more drawn to Chicago. He, however, had received a grant to take a year off from Virginia to go to Cambridge University to study George Boole, whose *Laws of Thought* had played a crucial role in the development of symbolic logic. To Robert Hutchins he wrote that he thought his work with Boole would be good preparation for liberal arts at Chicago. In April of 1931, before leaving for England, he wrote, "I am bored to death with everything."[3]

Cambridge did not serve to overcome his boredom. He had some interesting, but slow, conversations with G. E. Moore and a few fast and mutually provocative conversations with Wittgenstein. He attended a meeting of the British Association for the Advancement of Science at which J. J. Thomson, Millikan, Bohr, Jeans, and Eddington were present; Ed-

dington, according to his account, "put on the board a deduction he had made the night before of the velocity of the [receding] nebulae from Thomson's and Millikan's formula for the weight of an electron."[4] He met T. S. Eliot whom he described as "very agreeable but not much more"; Eliot gave him a letter of introduction to Jacques Maritain. The writing of a small volume called *Symbolic Distance* which pursued the theme of *Poetry and Mathematics,* was, he said, his "sheet anchor" at Cambridge. "Everything else," he wrote to Adler, "has gone bad, except possibly Bowes and Bowes bookshop."[5] He came to the conclusion that the decay of the intellectual arts had proceeded much farther in England than in the United States, and he attributed that to the Cambridge school of grammatical logic. Having received reports from Balz at Virginia that the philosophy faculty and students were responding to the new life brought there by Charles Davenport, F.S.C. Northrup, and himself, he found the prospect of returning not so cheerless, and wrote to Adler, "When I go back, I shall install the liberal arts in the school of philosophy or in a new honors school. Will you come to Virginia?"[6]

Back in Virginia in 1932, Buchanan became increasingly interested in medicine. This was an old interest that went back to his boyhood, when he used to go on sick calls with his father who was a physician in the little town of Jeffersonville, Vermont. It was enhanced by his view of the medieval university where, as he saw it, the faculties of medicine, law, and theology provided the subject matter that drew the greatest power from the liberal arts. As a consequence of this interest he obtained a leave of absence from Virginia for the second semester of the 1933-34 session to study the philosophy of medicine at the Johns Hopkins Medical School. Out of this study came *The Doctrine of Signatures*, a book which seeks to relate the liberal arts to the study of medicine. In the meantime he had been working on a more specific formulation of a plan for undergraduate education than anything he had produced before. In March 1934 he wrote to Adler from Baltimore that John Lloyd Newcomb, recently elected president of the University of Virginia, was "very much interested in my plan for general honors."[7] He complained, however, that Newcomb had double-crossed him because Newcomb had expressed to Barr a fear that "the requirements I had made in mathematics would scare the good students away and wreck the whole scheme. You see he objects to the quadrivium being an important part of the Liberal Arts, too. He must be an Aristotelian, but he didn't dare tell me." Of course, it is incorrect to say that Aristotle had little or no place for mathematics in education, though, to be sure, he does not present mathematics as a preparation for philosophy in the way Socrates does in Plato's *Republic,* Book VII.

On September 15, 1934, Newcomb appointed a committee of Virginia faculty to give their judgment on "the whole subject of honors courses." Robert Kent Gooch, professor of political science, was the chairman. Barr,

Shapiro Studio

Scott Buchanan.

Buchanan, J. J. Luck, and A. F. Benton were members; and also George O. Ferguson, dean of the college, was a member ex officio. At that time an undergraduate who met certain qualifications could in his third and fourth years select some special subject and work for "Final Honors" in that subject under the guidance of a faculty member who would direct his reading, assign him papers to write, and discuss them with him, usually at weekly meetings. The model for the honors courses was the 'tutorial' in the sense in which that word has been used in English universities, except that the student who read for final honors was also required to register for a certain number of lecture courses. The committee in the course of reviewing and appraising the honors courses, as Scott Buchanan recalled in 1962, went far beyond the original assignment.[8] In March of 1935 they submitted to President Newcomb a unanimous report which was a combination of the views of Buchanan and Gooch, who had been a Rhodes scholar and was very much an advocate of the freedom that the Oxford undergraduate has for study on his own.

The plan for the first two years, essentially Buchanan's, was in outline much the same as what later became the St. John's program. It set forth a design for the study and practice of the liberal arts through the reading and discussion of great books. The list of books by authors and their works was extremely close to the first such list as fashioned for the program at St. John's. The books were divided into two very general categories: 1) works of language and literature, and 2) works of mathematics and science. Each category included (a) works expository of the liberal arts; (b) exemplary models of the liberal arts; and (c) materials for analysis and practice in the liberal arts. These classifications were to appear in modified form in the second St. John's new program catalogue. The books were to be "read in their entirety and the maximum possible understanding achieved."

When one considers that the plan was to read in two years almost as many books as St. John's undergraduates now read in four years, and to read in their entirety books many of which are now read at St. John's only in part, and that the list contained Thomas Aquinas' *Summa Theologiae*, Part I, Newton's *Principia*, Kant's *Critique of Pure Reason*, Hegel's *Phenomenology*, Maxwell's *Treatise on Electricity and Magnetism*, etc., one sees the impossibility of the task. But the plan had not been put to the severe test of practice as it was to be later at St. John's. Only a few Platonic dialogues were included in the list, *Cratylus, Republic, Sophist,* and *Timaeus*, and only two works of Aristotle, the *Organon* and the *Poetics*. (In the first list proposed for St. John's there were only three Platonic dialogues, *Meno, Republic,* and *Sophist*, and the same two works of Aristotle). No work of Hobbes appears, and none of Locke's political writings.

The report affirmed as the end of education the formation of the intellectual virtues as described by Aristotle in Book VI of the *Ethics*, comprising

not only philosophical wisdom but also practical wisdom as right reason governing action and art as right reason governing making.[9] Liberal arts were to be the means to this end; the liberal arts that were "invented by the Greeks, but improved during the following twenty centuries." There was the following account of the liberal arts:

TRIVIUM
Grammar, the art and science of concrete things as they are used in mediums of expression.
Rhetoric, the art and science of applying such notations to things both concrete and abstract for practical and theoretical ends.
Logic, the art and science of discovering and applying abstract forms.

QUADRIVIUM
Arithmetic and **Geometry,** the mathematical arts and sciences that correspond to grammar in the Trivium.
Music, the art and science that deals with applied mathematics in all the natural sciences.
Astronomy, the art and science that deals with proportions, propositions, and proofs, including mathematical logic.

There were to be seminars, though they were not called that, for the discussion of the readings, two instructors for each seminar, tutorials in languages and mathematics for individuals or groups, as need might dictate, and a laboratory to perform the crucial experiments in the history of science, to practice the arts of measurement and experiment, and to illustrate scientific theory.

What was proposed for the third and fourth years, under the strong recommendation of Robert K. Gooch, was only a development of the already existing honors course. The student in those years was to be freed from all routine course requirements. He would be expected to work largely on his own to acquire a "relatively thorough mastery of one field of knowledge" instead of "course smatterings." The department or school, in which he would be enrolled for honors work, was to bear in mind, however, that the aim was liberal education rather than preparation for graduate work. Although the committee recommended the two proposals as an "integral whole", they were ready to allow exceptional students to be admitted to the honors course of the last two years even if they had not undergone the discipline of the first two.

By no means was it the intention of the committee that all the students

in the university's undergraduate college should follow this curriculum. It was intended for "a small group of picked students," for "the ablest students," for "the first-rate students," for "the best minds." Twenty-five years later Buchanan said that they had "hoped that the curriculum would finally be accepted by the whole college."[10] There is no indication of that hope in the report. On the contrary, the report shows clearly that at that time the proponents of this curriculum thought of it as being not for run-of-the-mill University students but for the gifted few.

For several months President Newcomb tried to obtain funds to get the curriculum started but was unable to do so. Even if it did not get started then at Virginia, the work that had gone into it was to bear fruit later at St. John's.

In October of the year the Virginia report was submitted, Adler made the suggestion that Stringfellow Barr be made dean of the college at Chicago and that Buchanan come to Chicago as a professor in the college. His suggesting Barr for dean was, as he wrote Buchanan, based on three things:

(1) He is sound about college education, as sound as anyone can be;
(2) He has guts of the kind Bob needs to put over the really radical program we have all been talking about;
(3) He is a man of character, a gentleman, and not a politician.[11]

Buchanan would have a better chance of seeing the liberal arts program put into effect if they came to Chicago than if they didn't. "You can't do the thing at Virginia," Adler wrote, "and you know it; you may not be able to do it here, but the chance with Winkie[12] as Dean and you and I and Arthur as professors in the College is pretty great." Buchanan replied that Barr was interested, that he himself was feeling "completely washed up" at Virginia and "completely washed up on academic philosophy," that if Barr could be persuaded to be dean at Chicago, Barr would be willing then to try to appoint him and that he would accept if he were still sane.[13] Less than a month later, again in a letter to Adler, he described his and Barr's situation as the "anomaly of serious conservatives in exile."[14] "I am terribly low," he wrote, "I have simply got to leave this place; suicide is the end from all these drifts of events if I don't manage to change things somehow." Newcomb was still trying to obtain financial support for the honors course, and Buchanan could add, "Supposing something happens, we may have some excitement about that."

Hutchins backed off from inviting Barr and Buchanan as dean and professor in the college. Very soon, however, Hutchins, together with Adler and McKeon, who had come in 1934 from Columbia, came up with a project which would get them to Chicago. This was the project for the formation of the Committee on the Liberal Arts, which had been made possible by a gift from Marion Rosenwald Stern, daughter of Julius Rosenwald. The committee were to think, talk, and write about the liberal arts, and perhaps

also do some lectures. The members were Adler, Barr, Buchanan, McKeon, and Rubin, together with certain junior members, R. Catesby Taliaferro and Charles Glenn Wallis, who had been students of Barr and Buchanan at Virginia, William Gorman, who had been at the Institute of Medieval Studies in Toronto, and several others. Buchanan was to be chairman.

The accounts of what happened when the committee began to meet conflict in several details. But they all agree that the enterprise blew up before it could really get started. The trio of Adler, Buchanan, and McKeon, who had been so close when they were in New York in the twenties and who in the early thirties had thought of themselves as working together to change American education, had moved apart intellectually. Adler had abandoned the position he had taken in *Dialectic*. *Dialectic* was a book that had been published in 1927 at the same time as Buchanan's *Possibility*. The two books had the same publisher and were advertised and reviewed together "As if they were Siamese twins," Adler has said.[15] And they were twins. *Dialectic* took the position of non-commitment to anything that might be called philosophical truth, as *Possibility* set forth a methodology for relating dialectically all systems of thought. Later Adler came to think that a philosopher must not only love or desire and seek truth, but find it; and he thought he had found important philosophical and theological truths in the writings of Aristotle and Thomas Aquinas. He saw McKeon as having taken up his own old way of thinking. "He can take any position," Adler wrote to Hutchins, "and justify it by interpreting it as one method of approaching the problem. This, it seems to me, is simply a way of avoiding the dilemma of having to decide which position is true, and which false."[16] He also thought of McKeon as having become more and more opposed to the religious implications of his own adherence to Thomistic doctrine. In some ways Buchanan was at this point closer intellectually to McKeon than he was to Adler, though his friendship with Adler was deeper, and he himself, without becoming a Thomist, had a special interest in Thomas Aquinas.[17] His opinion or feeling about McKeon was reflected in a letter he wrote Adler in November of 1935 in which he said, "He [Richard McKeon] feels that we have stolen the trivium and the quadrivium from his medieval safety box, and he is going to block us at every point in our attempts to use them, particularly if he is not the boss."[18] The way the relationships of the three had developed was not promising for the success of the Committee on Liberal Arts. According to Adler the committee as a whole had only a few meetings,[19] according to Buchanan, one meeting.[20] They did manage to agree on a text of Aristotle's to read and discuss together, but when they started their discussions, there were vehement accusations of distortion of the text. As Buchanan described the situation, "McKeon, Adler, and I, each of us, had constructed universes of discourse which reached into deep matters of method and metaphysics. The three worlds separately had absorbed and accumulated

the energies of our associates. They also carried within them the stresses and strains of our chaotic intellectual culture."[21] The committee fell apart, and the Virginia contingent with Buchanan at the head proceeded to read and discuss great books and to develop the plan that had been contained in the Virginia report. Barr claims that it was the reading of Plato's *Dialogues* and Euclid's *Elements* during this year at Chicago that finally won him over to trying to do something to bring into being the program which Buchanan, with his encouragement, had been planning over the years. He has said that it was the reading of these works that made him accept the presidency of St. John's in 1937.[22]

Sometime in May of that year Francis Sayre, then assistant secretary of state and son-in-law of Woodrow Wilson, together with Alexander C. Zabriskie, professor of church history at the Episcopal Seminary in Alexandria, Virginia, Henry Pitt vanDusen, president of Union Theological Seminary in New York and Francis Pickens Miller, then a member of the Virginia House of Delegates, assembled at the Alexandria seminary a group of twelve people to discuss the increasingly ominous international situation. Scott Buchanan was one of the twelve and shared with Francis Miller an attic room in the home of Charles Lowry, professor of theology. Miller had recently become a member of the board of St. John's College. He described the desperate state of the college to Buchanan. They talked on and on, and even after retiring to bed in the darkness of the attic room they continued to talk about education and St. John's College. The upshot of this nocturnal conversation was that Buchanan promised that he would see if he couldn't persuade Hutchins to leave the University of Chicago and become president of St. John's. Upon returning to Chicago he tried and failed to persuade Hutchins. Then he talked to Barr. He and Barr agreed that their future in Chicago did not seem promising. The strong opposition of most of the University of Chicago faculty and the strong departmental organization had made it difficult for Hutchins to put into effect whatever opinions he shared with Barr and Buchanan about liberal arts education. The Committee on the Liberal Arts had itself fallen apart. Barr and Buchanan were assured of only one more year at Chicago. They thought that, if they meant what they had been saying about liberal education, they ought to do something now that the opportunity had come.

They met with the whole board of St. John's on June 4th at the University Club in Baltimore. The board did not begin the interview with such questions as who would be president, what salary he might ask, or what his chances might be for raising the funds that the college so urgently needed. Instead, they wanted, first of all, to talk about education and the program that Barr and Buchanan would introduce if they were to accept appointment by the board. That, of course, was very encouraging to them. Richard Cleveland, son of Grover Cleveland, an intelligent, able, and public-spirited

Baltimore lawyer, was chairman of the board's presidential search committee and had played a key role in arousing initial interest in the proposed program among members of the board. He, no doubt, contributed much to the tone and the course of the discussion. As Buchanan described this event, "We sat and explained the program that we would put in. We didn't discuss anything else until we did get that across. How much they understood, of course, was very difficult to know, but they were impressed. And I felt that somehow we had come to terms with them."[23]

The board, convinced of the worth of the program, also saw that in order to put it into operation Barr and Buchanan would have to have the authority they were then asking for. An agreement was made that they could employ whatever means they considered most suitable for what they hoped to accomplish, and the board would not interfere. At the same time, they, on their part, agreed that they would resign on twenty-four hours' notice, if the board should request their resignations. Cleveland recommended that Barr be elected president and stated, "If elected, he [Barr] would understand that the Board desires to undertake at St. John's the liberal arts course which he describes, and that this course shall, as soon as practicable, become a major concern of the College. The Committee believes that the Board should deliberately recognize the implications of this commitment, and should not elect Mr. Barr unless they feel wholeheartedly in sympathy with his purpose and unless they are prepared to give him support in the undertaking, and accept his understanding of his function."[24] The board on June 18th proceeded to elect Barr as president, having incorporated in the resolution for his election the understanding expressed in the committee's report.

Barr, having accepted the presidency, then recommended the appointment of Buchanan as dean. At the same time they appointed Buchanan they elected Barr and Robert M. Hutchins to the board. At that time the president of the college was not a board member. Buchanan was not elected to the board until March 8, 1938. Since then both the president and the dean (now the two deans for the two campuses) have been board members ex officio.

In order that everyone would be clear about what had been agreed on, Barr, in accepting the presidency, wrote a letter to the board in which he stated that by electing him they were electing a program of education, that it would be his function to instruct the faculty and the trustees in the program, that it would be his duty to make practical decisions involving students, faculty, trustees, and the public. He concluded, "If the public is to be educated up to an understanding of our program, and if the necessary funds are to be worth raising, it is, I repeat, imperative that the President and the Board keep that program continuously and clearly in mind as their common objective. This program is not the introduction of another 'experiment' into an educational system already disorganized by expediency and com-

placency. It is the restoration of St. John's to the great and ancient tradition of liberal education. I must apologize if, in my effort to make this letter brief, I have appeared brusque or presumptuous. I have sought to avoid presumption by speaking not of myself as a person . . . but of a program which, here or elsewhere, will mark an important day in American education."[25]

The appointment of Barr and Buchanan and the program they were bringing to St. John's immediately received wide publicity. On July 11 the Baltimore *Sun* published an article by Barr in which he described the program in terms of the great books and the liberal arts. One thing he said was quite different from what had been said in the Virginia report, namely, that the program "is not conceived as only for the better students, but rather as the common intelligible way of learning for both good and mediocre minds. It has become a common saying with us that the duller minds need the best material even more than the best minds do."[26] He also said, "It is our ambition to set up a model for other American colleges to follow." For the educational principles underlying the new plan at St. John's he referred the reader to Robert Hutchins's *The Higher Learning in America*. Hutchins himself in an interview a few days earlier had said that he had accepted membership on the St. John's board "in order to assist in a revival of the ancient purposes of education" and suggested that "the changes about to be made at St. John's might be a turning point in American educational history" and that St. John's was "an excellent place to try out the idea of educating people to live instead of to earn a living."[27]

The Higher Learning in America, originally given as the Stowe lectures at Yale, and published as a book in 1936, shows the influence of Buchanan and Adler on Hutchins's views about education. It deplores the notion that education is for the sake of "commodious living," or that it consists in training for a vocation. It also criticizes American colleges and universities for their fragmentation into departments with consequent disunity and lack of communication. Just as in the Virginia report, the end of education is said to be the five intellectual virtues as defined by Aristotle and understood to be good in themselves. Great books and discipline in the liberal arts of grammar, rhetoric, logic, and mathematics are recommended as means for reforming American education. But much more weight is placed on the revitalization and restoration of metaphysics for the establishment of first principles to give unity to all the sciences and the whole educational enterprise in the way theology did in the Middle Ages. No specific metaphysics is advocated. Nevertheless, metaphysics is conceived as a science that starts from first principles. Subordinate to metaphysics in the university would be the study of man in the social sciences—ethics, politics, and economics—and the study of nature in the natural sciences. All of this is very much like the way Buchanan imagined the faculties of law and medicine as subordinate

to the faculty of theology (with philosophy as handmaid) in the medieval university.

Although neither Barr nor Buchanan subscribed to everything in Hutchins's book, Barr recommended it in order to provide a more complete account of the principles underlying the new program at St. John's than could be given in a newspaper article. As yet very little that was specific had been made public. Early in August 1937, however, Scott Buchanan issued a supplement to the St. John's catalogue which set forth in detail what the curriculum was to be. In broad outline it was to be the curriculum delineated in the Virginia report. But for the first time Buchanan stated five criteria for a 'great book':

(1) It is a book that has been read by the largest number of persons. (By this he did not mean a book that might appear on a current bestseller list, but rather a book like the Bible or some of Shakespeare's plays that have, over the centuries, had more readers than other books, and that have "stood the test of time").

(2) It is a book that has the greatest number of alternative, independent, and consistent interpretations. (He did not mean a simply ambiguous book. "A really ambiguous book," he said, "has no meaning or interpretation." Dante's *Comedy* and Newton's *Principia* were given as examples of books with multiple interpretations).

(3) It raises the persistent unanswerable questions.[28] (He cited as such questions those about "number and measurement, matter and form, ultimate substance, tragedy, and God").

(4) It must be a work of fine art. (By this he meant that it has an immediate intelligibility because of its beauty in the sense of "order, elegance, and effulgence of form").

(5) It must be a masterpiece of the liberal arts.

If one were to apply these criteria to each of the books in the list that accompanied Buchanan's statement, one would surely find that very few meet all of them. But it can be said that every book on the list meets one or more of them.

During the summer in which this supplement to the catalogue appeared, Buchanan wrote a long essay which bore the title "In Search of a Liberal College."[29] The phrase "in search of a liberal college" was one that he was to use often later in life to convey how he understood what he had been engaged in at St. John's. It indicates that he did not think of himself and those associated with him as being in possession of a blueprint for the perfect liberal arts college. While presenting Plato, Aristotle, and Thomas Aquinas as masters of the exposition of the liberal arts, he could say, "I hold no dogmatic brief for the language of Plato, Aristotle, and the Middle Ages. There may be a better language in which these fundamental educational matters can be discussed and expounded. But I know of none better." He

saw the classics as the "largest and most imposing symbolic constructions the European animal has made." For that reason he recognized a danger in the study of Aristotle, the danger that the list would become "commentary material on Aristotle." "There has been a tendency in that direction at Chicago," he said. He thought of the great books as being essentially interrelated: "In order to understand any great book it would seem wise to read all the great books that have gone into its making . . . The best commentaries, introductions, handbooks, and purveyors for a great book are other great books." He anticipated a danger that subsequently has concerned critics and friends of St. John's: "The danger in the whole St. John's program is dilettantism, the organization of a scheme that at first hearing sounds formalistic and rigoristic, as well as romantic, whose failures will be dilettantism and sophistry."

Toward the close of this essay Buchanan, with a characteristic flair for surprising suggestions, invited the reader "to think in as free a way as possible about the whole St. John's proposal on two backgrounds: for the past, the Benedictine monastery with its useful, liberal, and divine arts and their rotating daily schedule; for the future the cinematic institute where mathematical physics finds a liberal home and progressively finds the synthesis for what may be a twentieth-century renaissance of the same useful, liberal, and divine arts." At the beginning of the essay he had pictured the Benedictine monastery as the one institution which in the past had most successfully combined the three kinds of arts. Near the end he suggested that there should be at St. John's an Institute of Cinematics which would be a research institute, separate from, but in close relationship with, the undergraduate curriculum, where movies would be made and "everything from the raw material, both animate and inanimate, to the finished movie performance, [would be] studied from both theoretical and practical standpoints." "The movies, " he claimed, "put all the arts together. In some sense they offer the only major activity of modern civilization which properly and exhaustively mirrors the liberal college."

Barr and Buchanan continued to resist the portrayal of the program as experimental. From their point of view, even if they were in search of the liberal college, they had discovered enough in the tradition of liberal education to claim that they were restoring something that had already been tested and found good rather than experimenting with something to see whether it would prove good. In an address in August 1937 on "Reviewing the Ancient Purpose of Education" Barr stated, "True liberal education is one of the few things in life that can never be called an experiment."[30] In 1966 Buchanan in retrospect said, "I think we were a little purist, a little pedantic in saying we were not experimenting. We had a program, and we thought it was near enough right so you'd try to do it and not take measurements every day to see if it were working. In that sense, we were not experimen-

tal. We were trying to do something with great determination and it would take some time to see whether it could be done."[31]

Barr and Buchanan were now ready to do something they had long been dreaming of. They had the authority they needed; the board had agreed that, except in an extreme and unlikely situation, when the board might ask for Barr's resignation, he would be in charge and not the board. There could be no college, however, without faculty and students. Would the faculty already at the college welcome the new program? What new faculty might there be? Should the elective system be continued for students enrolled in the upper classes? Who would be the students in the new program? Would all the insight and determination of Buchanan and Barr result in its becoming an effective means of education for those students?

CHAPTER 3

The New Program at St. John's

On September 22, 1937, forty-five freshmen, of whom twenty had enrolled in the new program, marched in procession from the St. John's Library to McDowell Hall for the Convocation ceremony in which their formal matriculation was completed. Dr. Amos Hutchins, a Baltimore physician and loyal alumnus (not related to Robert Hutchins), then chairman of the board, presided. Richard Cleveland addressed the assembled faculty and students. He told them that he and his fellow board members had the greatest confidence in Barr and his associates, and that the new program was not a new departure for the college but was in accord with its charter of 1784 which sets as the purpose of the college "the liberal education of youth in the principles of virtue, knowledge, and useful literature" and "instruction in all liberal arts, and sciences and in the ancient and modern tongues and languages."[1]

The old program was being continued for students in the sophmore, junior, and senior classes, and the freshmen were for the last time being allowed to choose between the old program and the new so that by 1941 the old program would be gone. Of the twenty freshmen who chose the new program, nine had already attended St. John's for one or more years but were happy to begin again as freshmen, so strongly were they attracted by the program now being introduced. The initial response of the students was favorable to the new president and the new dean and their plans. The *Collegian,* the student newspaper, which had been started in 1888, addressed an open letter to them in the name of the whole student body in an issue that appeared the day before Convocation.

> What we are most grateful for [the letter said] is your plan of education, your so-called "New Program" which offers such an opportunity for a student to test his mettle and to gain incalculably by so doing. We realize that this is but the beginning, that no one can say what changes will be necessary in the future,

but we believe in the basic idea of a return to original great thought in a coordinated fashion.[2]

At the meeting of the board in January 1938, Barr could report that he had never before in his academic career known a situation like that at St. John's where freshmen of average backgrounds were working hard on Greek and Euclidean geometry and eagerly reading Plato. He claimed that there was already convincing evidence of what could be done if the end of liberal education were clearly defined and if all means available were directed to that end.[3] Shortly after that a reporter from the Baltimore *Sun* visited the campus and interviewed several students.[4] He found that, as Barr had told the board, the students were working very hard and at the same time were finding pleasure in what they were learning. A representative comment was that of John O. Neustadt, a junior who had elected to become a freshman again and who was quoted as saying: "Those great books are damned good — there's no getting around that — no matter who teaches them. But the way these fellows take them up here, you see something you never thought was there."

Shortly after becoming president, Barr had assembled in his office the incumbent faculty members who were in Annapolis that summer. This was before he had made any announcement to the press about the form and content of the curriculum. There were only about twenty-five faculty members in all. He explained to those assembled that there were three groups of the faculty: (1) those who would be interested in the program and would teach successfully in it; (2) those who would be interested but who, for one reason or another, would find that they could not be successful teachers in the new curriculum; and (3) those who would not be at all interested and would prefer to leave and teach elsewhere. He promised help in finding employment for all who might want to leave or might have to be dropped. There was nothing in the way of organized opposition from the faculty as there might have been in a college or university where there were strong departments. Because of such opposition Hutchins had been unable to accomplish at Chicago the changes he thought desirable. Some of the faculty left right away, some stayed for a few years, and four continued to the end of their teaching careers: George Bingley, a mathematician; Ford Brown, a former Rhodes scholar and an authority on the Evangelicals in the Church of England; Richard Scofield, another Rhodes scholar who had previously taught art and English and very quickly proved the breadth of his interest and ability by the excellence of his teaching within the new program; and John Kieffer, in whom the program got a warm welcome because of his background in classical languages and literature.

It was, however, important for Barr and Buchanan to have with them some who had already had some familiarity with their plans and some ex-

Alfred Eisenstaedt/Life Magazine

Seminar led by Scott Buchanan (upper left).

perience with teaching the kind of curriculum they envisaged. They brought with them from Chicago James S. Martin, R. Catesby Taliaferro, and Charles Glenn Wallis. Martin had been in a Hutchins-Adler great books seminar as an undergraduate at Chicago and subsequently had graduated from the Chicago Law School. He was appointed to teach history and government to old program students with the intention that he would later be available for the new program. Taliaferro and Wallis had both come under Buchanan's spell at Virginia, Taliaferro having received his doctorate in philosophy there in 1936 and Wallis his B.A. with Final Honors in philosophy the same year. They had gone with Barr and Buchanan to Chicago to be members of the Committee on the Liberal Arts, and now they accompanied them to Annapolis. Taliaferro was a stickler for discipline in his language and mathematics tutorials. He believed that the seminar discussions would become mere "tea-table talk" without extensive and intensive drilling in languages and mathematics, and he acted accordingly. In the tutorials he would pace up and down the floor with a cane; contrary to rumor, he never used the cane on a student. In the seminar discussions he was nothing of the martinet. There was no question of drilling there. He did not seek to indoctrinate. He knew better than to suppose that one could teach Plato by drilling students in Socratic arguments. His own enthusiasm and capacity for hard work impressed and inspired his students. Wallis had as a schoolboy at The Donaldson School near Baltimore learned Greek and Latin. He continued with Greek and Latin at the University of Virginia, and then began the study of philosophy under Buchanan.

Taliaferro and Wallis performed a notable service to the program by translating into English certain books of which there were at that time no available complete translations. Taliaferro translated the first three books of Apollonius' *Conics* and Ptolemy's *Almagest*; Wallis put into English Copernicus' *De Revolutionibus Orbium Caelestium,* part of Kepler's *Epitome,* and other books. These translations were all finished within two years after the program was introduced and left something to be desired because of the rapidity with which they had to be produced and also because of the difficulties intrinsic to the texts. Wallis would no doubt have improved his translation of Copernicus had he not met an untimely death by falling out of a window in Manhattan.

A somewhat unexpected boon to the program was the appointment of George Comenetz. Buchanan went to his friend, Edward Kasner, professor of mathematics at Columbia and asked him, "Who is your best recent Ph.D. in mathematics?" Kasner unhesitatingly replied, "George Comenetz." Comenetz had been for two years at the Institute for Advanced Study at Princeton after he got his degree at Columbia. When he came to St. John's, Buchanan, who already knew what mathematical classics he wanted to have studied, assigned him the task of planning in detail just what would be read and

when in the works of Euclid, Apollonius, Ptolemy, Copernicus, Descartes, Galileo, Newton, etc. This task he carried out judiciously, and the result is still recognizable in the first three years of the mathematics program. Comenetz also wrote several short texts to assist the students in understanding the mathematical classics. He once said to me regretfully, "There is one important thing that is missing, and that is Einstein's special theory of relativity, but it is too difficult for our students." It was only much later that a way was found to make not only Einstein's theory, but Einstein's own very condensed 1905 paper, accessible to St. John's students.

Comenetz was also charged with organizing the laboratory for the freshman year. Buchanan is his essay *In Search of a Liberal College* had sketched a plan for the laboratory: first year, instruments of scientific method; second and third years, crucial experiments from the great books (as, for example, Galileo's *Two New Sciences* and Huygen's *On Light*); fourth year, biological and medical science with special concentration on the nature of the cell. It fell to Comenetz that first year of the program to plan a sequence of laboratory exercises that would explore basic questions about the measurement of fundamental physical quantities such as length, area, volume, time, weight, density, temperature, and heat. He found this harder than designing in detail the mathematics program, but his care and diligence produced experiments that raised basic questions in physics and made it possible for students to explore them.

Whether or not it was because he was a mathematician by training, George Comenetz's teaching was characterized by the utmost economy of speech. He never wasted a word, but he always said enough. According to his students, he never made a mistake when presenting a mathematical proof or something similar in class. He also had a nice sense of humor.

This author first met him on a visit to St. John's in the spring of 1940, while attending a class of his in Ptolemy. He was using a model that Taliaferro had made of the Ptolemaic world. He turned a crank and asked, "What's that?" The students replied in unison, "The motion of the same." He turned another crank and asked, "What's that?" They replied in unison, "The motion of the other." He asked, "Who am I?" The response came, again in unison, "God." He said, "Or at least a soul." Later I was to learn how fundamental "the motion of the same" and "the motion of the other," so named in Plato's *Timaeus,* are for the understanding of ancient astronomy and hence of the roots of modern astronomy.

It has often been said that the seminar is the heart of the St. John's program and that the tutorials and the laboratory are for the sake of the seminar. Buchanan was the principal seminar leader for the first new program students, and he went right through the four years of seminars with them. It is almost incredible how much he did in the first year of his deanship. Not only was he leading the student seminar, he was also conducting a

Alfred Eisenstaedt/Life Magazine

Stringfellow Barr.

separate seminar in great books for faculty members and at a certain point a seminar for the wives of faculty. Many a night he was up until long after midnight reading great books, some of which he had never read before. All this was in addition to his special duties as dean. Looking back after nearly thirty years, he said that he could hardly believe that he had undertaken to conduct seminars for faculty members about whose reappointments he would have to make recommendations to Barr.[5] "But," he commented, "we did read the books, and we discussed them fairly well — we had real seminar quarrels with each other — long arguments."[6]

One of the slogans of the college during those early years of the program was: "The great books are the teachers." Buchanan meant that. He considered the faculty relatively unimportant. They were older students who were learning with other students and who might, because of special experience or training, help the others to learn. Adler on the occasion of one of his many visits to the college during the academic year 1937-38 gave, at Buchanan's request, a talk to the faculty on the desirability of incompetence in a college teacher. The point was that, if a teacher begins to think of himself as an expert and ceases to reexamine what he is teaching, he loses the awareness of his ignorance and becomes a sophist.

Buchanan was himself a remarkable teacher. In *Embers of the World* he says something about what he thinks teaching is: "I think teaching is primarily the business of listening to the pupil and responding to whatever happens in the pupil with further questions, and it could be that the questions were statements. I mean statements are questions if you understand them properly. A statement is saying, 'Well, what do you think of this?' " Buchanan was the sort of teacher he describes. He was a patient listener, always attentive to a student's questions, sometimes transforming them into questions the student hadn't asked but wished he had. He was good at asking the right questions at the right times and at presenting statements in such a way that they would not be taken as final answers but as provoking or leading to further questions. People have compared him to Socrates. But to say that he was like Socrates does not do him justice. He delighted in taking extreme positions, in arousing thought by making startling analogies from which he would draw the most far-reaching consequences, in trying to reconcile the irreconcilable. His tone of voice, his manner, his laugh, were all factors in the influence he had on those who came under his spell. His penetrating look made one think he could see into one's soul.

His intellectual interests were vast. They were primarily philosophical and theological. He knew, however, that one cannot seek wisdom as the philosopher does or seek understanding of the meaning and implications of what is given to faith without the rational investigation of human life and the world of which human life is a part. It was clear to him that for one to philosophize or to be a theologian demands more than a little acquaintance with poetry and with mathematics and science.

He was in no way bound by the inherited works of great thinkers. In some sense, though it seems strange, he did not really respect the authors of the great books; that is, he did not think it of first importance to try to find out exactly what the authors meant. In *Possibility* there are two chapters on Kant and Aristotle in which he seeks to isolate "those parts of their systems" that may be taken as foundations of methodology. These chapters are introduced by a three-page note entitled "Apology for Historical Piracy" in which he defends himself in advance against the charge of having misread or misinterpreted Kant and Aristotle. He says, "The realism that demands what Kant and Aristotle really meant when they said certain things is quite irrelevant to our purpose."[7] He could, therefore, like a pirate, plunder from both whatever might appear as a treasure that would be useful for the development of his own thought.

That he might as a consequence overlook or fail to find a greater treasure seems not to have occurred to him. He had an extraordinary ability to identify the books that contain treasures, but often did not recognize the treasures in them. In a conversation reported in *Embers of the World,* after maintaining that there is no doctrine in Plato's Socratic dialogues, not even in the *Republic,* he speaks rather slightingly of Plato's other dialogues in which "someone else takes the place of Socrates and there's no real discussion."[8] *Poetry and Mathematics* in a very imaginative passage reproduces in a nondeductive way almost the whole content of the first book of Euclid, so that one understands all that one needs for the proof of the famous Pythagorean Theorem.[9] Yet the same book provides instances of simple blunders that Buchanan would not have made had he been less cavalier in the way he read the great books.[10] For example, he attributes to Aristotle the proposition that the time (rather than the speed) of a body's fall is proportional to its weight, and to Galileo the proposition that the velocities acquired by a falling body accelerated from rest are as the squares of the distances of fall (rather than that the distances are as the squares of the times). In *Embers of the World* he sets out to state Thomas Aquinas' order of charity.[11] He gets it right up to a point. According to Thomas, the proper order of charity is this: One loves God first and above all else, then one's own soul, then one's neighbor's soul, then one's own body. "Our neighbor's body," he says, "is not reckoned as a special object of love . . . every man is immediately concerned with his own body, but not with his neighbor's welfare except perhaps in cases of urgency."[12] Buchanan, however, represents Thomas as putting in the fourth place after the love of God, of one's soul, and of one's neighbor's soul, the love of one's neighbor's body, and in a fifth place the love of one's own body. The difference is not such a trivial one since what Thomas says raises in a telling way the question of what kinds of action are demanded by the love of other human beings; in a way hardly fashionable today it places all the emphasis on doing what is for the good of one's

neighbor's soul, not on what one might do for the well-being of one's neighbor's body.

These are only a few examples, taken more or less at random, of out-and-out mistakes that Buchanan made about what the great books say. He might answer that being mistaken about what a book says is of little consequence and that what comes first in liberal education is the liberal arts as forms of thinking. He used to say of the liberal arts that no one of them has any specific content and that each has everything as its content. It is not so difficult to see how this might be true for the arts of the trivium: grammar, rhetoric, and logic are embodied in all written or spoken language, and if language has everything as its content, so do they. It is not so easy to see how it is true in the case of the arts of the quadrivium: arithmetic, geometry, music (harmonics), and astronomy. But from Buchanan's account of them in the Virginia report one perceives that he meant by those arts something nobody else had ever meant.[13] He was a man of the post-Cartesian world in that he was seeking methods and formulas and symbolic structures for learning or philosophizing, methods that would, he hoped, bring together the most diverse worlds of thought and imagination. One observes this in *Possibility,* which tries to formulate a methodology for accomplishing just this unity. One observes it in *Poetry and Mathematics* and *Symbolic Distance,* where analogical reasoning and insight are made the key to "treating poetry mathematically and mathematics poetically, to show the mutual reflections and common illuminations they afford." A favorite dictum of Buchanan's was: "All predications are analogical." Mortimer Adler in his autobiography tells an amusing, though for him sad, story of how, as he and Buchanan drew farther apart in the way they understood philosophizing, their conversations would become more and more confused.[14] Every time he would speak a sentence with the word "is", Buchanan thought he meant "is like", and every time Buchanan would use "is", Adler thought he meant "is" and not "is like". An illustration of what Adler was recalling was given me in a story told by Richard Scofield. In the first year of the program Buchanan gave a lecture in which he asserted, "Medea is the Virgin Mary." Adam Alles, who had been the philosophy department under the old regime, was exasperated, failing to see that "is" only meant "is like".[15] The following week the lecturer was a Dominican from Catholic University, Father Slavin, to whom in the question period after the lecture Alles quite out of the blue directed the question "Father, do you think Medea is the Virgin Mary?" The blackfriar was nonplussed, the dean angry.

One finds a similar concern about a method of philosophizing in Buchanan's doctrine of the transcendentals. The transcendentals are six terms of which some medieval thinkers said that they can be predicated of everything, of themselves, and of one another: one, being, true, good, thing (res), and something (aliquid). Buchanan claimed (and this was character-

istic) that he had gone a step farther to say that they can be predicated also of their opposites: many, non-being, false, evil; he maintained that "thing" and "something" are opposites of each other, identifying them sometimes with "same" and "other", sometimes with "universal" and "particular". In a course in metaphysics at Virginia in 1934-35 he proceeded to develop and to elaborate all the possible predications that arise when one says the transcendentals of themselves, of one another, and of their opposites:

> One is one.
> Being is one.
> The true is good.
> The good is something.
> One is many.
> The true is false.
> Evil is good. etc.

As he did this he would run through the history of philosophy, explicating the thought of every thinker in transcendental propositions. "The whole history of metaphysics," he claimed, "can be constructed out of these terms. The history of thought when looked at from the transcendental predicates can be said to be the history of the abduction of reason by them. They are the cause of reason's running away into infinities and paradoxes, and they will probably be the solution."[16]

Albert Balz once remarked, "For Scott Buchanan everything is true." A related comment was made by a young tutor who was co-leader one year with Buchanan in a St. John's seminar, "It is impossible to disagree with Buchanan." With his own methodology, by continuous use of analogy to bridge huge differences of thought, by predicating the transcendentals of one another and their opposites, Buchanan would reconcile irreconcilables. One might think one was disagreeing with him only to find, perhaps right away, perhaps only much later, that by some dialectical maneuver he had managed to embrace your side of the argument along with his. In a report to Hutchins just after he left Chicago for St. John's he wrote,

> Orthodoxy and heresy are both within the tradition or perhaps one can go so far as to say that heresy falls within orthodoxy as a part of it, and a vital part at that. This makes Mortimer creep when I say it to him but the difficulty is only verbal, I think. He thinks of heresy as contradictory to orthodoxy whereas it is either subalternate or subcontrary, and it is necessary if the orthodogma is to have its continued incarnation or is to be known by men. Orthodoxy and heresy are to the tradition what form and matter are to material substance in Aristotle's physics.[17]

It is no wonder that the first students, as well as most of the first faculty, in the new program and those who followed them in the later thirties and in the forties were intrigued and excited by this man who led them to think about things they had never thought about before, to wonder what it means to say that being is one or how being or truth might be good or evil, and to explore such questions in the course of reading Homer, Greek tragedies, or Platonic dialogues, to entertain the most startling analogies, and to combine heresy with orthodoxy. During the first year the first new program students through their seminars with Buchanan became more and more attracted to the dialogues and by the end of the year had read all the Platonic dialogues except *The Laws* instead of only the four that he had planned for them to read as expository of the liberal arts.

Buchanan's original plan for the language tutorials was to require a study of four foreign languages: Greek, Latin, French, and German in the four years respectively. The students were not expected to become proficient in any of these languages. It was expected, however, that by spending six or eight weeks memorizing paradigms, rules of syntax, and certain passages of good poetry and prose, they would be able to move toward a knowledge of universal grammar as a liberal art and to greater skill in reading and writing, and would be able to check their translations of the great books against the original texts. Time was then to be spent on the close analysis of texts, whether translations or original English texts, with a view to discovering not only the grammatical but also the rhetorical and logical patterns in them. In the third term (there were then three terms during the academic session) they were to write grammatical, rhetorical, and logical commentaries on the texts. This plan became somewhat modified when Catesby Taliaferro and John Kieffer persuaded the dean that for the ends he had in view more time for Greek and more conventional drill would be needed.[18] The result was that the whole first year in the language tutorial came to be allotted to learning Greek and to translating and analyzing the argument of Plato's *Meno*.

Translating a large section of the *Meno* has remained until the present time a part of the freshman's learning experience.

While the pattern became established for the freshman language tutorial and similar patterns for the language tutorials of the other years, there was still a great deal of variety in the actual teaching of the tutorials. In regard to this, Barr, reminiscing with Buchanan in 1966, said, "The formal arrangement of the curriculum misled a lot of people into not knowing that the variety the elective system tried to express was there all the time. In all of it. Although everyone did 'the same thing' and this enabled the students to have a common experience, but common *au fond*, it was not common superficially. There was a great deal of flexibility inside a very formal arrangement."[19]

What has been said about Buchanan's way of philosophizing should be

of help in understanding what his conception of the program was, why with all its emphasis on tradition it was not in any way committed to the past as past or to the thought of any particular thinker, why it was as ambitious as it was, and why it might be called philosophical in a large sense. Just as Buchanan himself was not particularly concerned to discover an author's meaning, neither was he particularly concerned that that should be the aim of the students. He expected them to get from their reading some thoughts, some insights, some questions which, though they might even spring from a serious misreading, would spark discussion and result in whatever the free intellect might thereby learn. No doubt, a seminar discussion would always begin with a question which would be related to the reading assignment for that seminar but it would not necessarily remain with the text. There was a phrase Buchanan liked: "following the argument where it leads." To read great texts was essential. It was equally essential that the intellect be free from the pedantry that results if it is too much bound by them. Perhaps Buchanan did not take seriously enough the danger of superficiality and dilettantism that might come from playing fast and loose with the thoughts of the great thinkers. He surely recognized that danger. Above all, he knew that thought is not identical with rethinking the thoughts of others.

CHAPTER 4

Public Interest and Internal Changes Under Barr and Buchanan

The St. John's curriculum, differing so radically from the curriculums of most American colleges, evoked widespread interest as soon as it was inaugurated. In December 1938 Walter Lippmann wrote a column that appeared in many newspapers in which he praised the St. John's way. He praised it primarily because it promised a recovery of an understanding of the principles on which the American Republic was founded, the understanding that the founding fathers had because of their own study of the classics. "I do know," he wrote, "that in this country and abroad there are men who see that the onset of barbarism must be met not only by programs of rearmament, but by another revival of learning. It is the fact, moreover, that after tentative beginnings in several of the American universities, Columbia, Virginia, and Chicago, a revival is actually begun — is not merely desired, talked about, and projected, but is in operation with teachers and students and a carefully planned course of study." He concluded with the prophecy: "I venture to believe that . . . in the future men will point to St. John's College and say that there was the seed-bed of the American Renaissance."[1]

There were many who wanted to know about the revival as it was in operation. A series of articles in the Baltimore *Sun* in January 1939 gave vignettes of what was going on in the tutorials.[2] The freshmen in their mathematics tutorial were wrestling with some of the most fundamental questions in mathematics raised by their investigation of book 5 of Euclid in the context of the discovery of incommensurable magnitudes. The same freshmen in their language tutorial were making careful analyses of Greek sentences and were translating Plato's *Meno*, using the Greek they were learning to try to find out what was happening in that dialogue, why Socrates said what he said, or asked what he asked, and what Meno's answers might mean in the development of the dialogue. The sophmores were enthusiastically engaged with Apollonius' *Conics*, being in a position to contemplate the beautiful logical and analogical structure of the first book of that work, which they had recently finished reading. In their language tutorial they

were translating from a chapter of Augustine's *Confessions,* and producing the following: "They [Augustine's friends who wanted him to write the book] are desirous to hear me confess what I am within: whither neither eye, nor ear, nor understanding is able to divine; they desire it as ready to believe me; but will they know me?" This led to a lively discussion of Augustine's effort at self-knowledge and of whether one can know oneself thoroughly.

About a year later *Life* magazine sent to the college Gerard Piel, who later became the founder and publisher of *Scientific American.*[3] Piel brought with him the photographer, Alfred Eisenstadt, and together they produced with words and pictures a quite accurate and attractive account of St. John's with the new program in operation. There was a picture of Buchanan leading a seminar, of a student, Francis Mason, in rapt contemplation of one of Euclid's regular solids, of a group of students in the snow using an instrument with which Aristarchus (third century BC) made measurements from which to calculate the sizes and distances of the sun and moon. A two-page spread showed a shelf of the great books with those translated by St. John's faculty clearly marked. These pictures and the accompanying story, both concise and complete, gave a great boost to the enrollment. In the fall of 1940 ninety-three freshmen enrolled as contrasted with forty in 1938 and fifty-four in 1939. People sometimes referred to the class of 1944 as the "*Life* class."

As a visitor to the college in the spring of 1940 I was especially struck by the amount of activity on the part of students in every class, not simply in the seminars where it was to be expected. But for the whole college community there were also formal lectures which in the first few years of the new program occurred sometimes as often as twice a week, although fairly soon the one lecture on Friday became, as it has remained, the custom. These lectures were given by St. John's faculty members and also by visiting lecturers, and were followed by lively question periods. The first one of the year was always given by Buchanan and was about the liberal arts. Many of the lectures had to do with the liberal arts and reflected Buchanan's view that the main thing in education is the liberal arts and that great books are material for the exercise of those arts. Adler and Meiklejohn were officially named "Lecturers," and were listed in the catalogue as members of the faculty. For quite a while Adler came once a month from Chicago and lectured on two successive days on such topics as "The Liberal Arts—Master and Student," "Symbols," and "Terms." Meiklejohn visited the college every spring and would stay for several weeks, lecturing and meeting with small groups to discuss Kant. As a result of his persuasion, supported by a very sharp intelligence, many students came to see Kant as a viable option. For several years it was his assignment at the commencement exercises to read a favorite passage from the apocryphal book of 1st Esdras, the passage in which three young men in the presence of King Darius engage in a com-

Alfred Eisenstaedt/Life Magazine

Francis S. Mason, Jr. with Euclidean solid.

petition of wise sentences about "the strongest of things." One says, "Wine is the strongest of all things." Another says, "The king is the strongest." The third says, "Women are the strongest," but then begins a retraction:

> O ye men are not women strong? Great is the earth, high is the heaven, swift is the sun in his course, for he compasseth the heaven round about, and fetcheth his course again to his own place in one day.
>
> Is he not great that maketh these things? Therefore great is the truth and stronger than all things.
>
> All the earth calleth upon the truth, and the heaven blesseth it: all works shake and tremble at it and with it is no unrighteous thing.
>
> Wine is wicked, the king is wicked, women are wicked, and all the children of men are wicked and such are all their wicked works; and there is no truth in them; in their unrighteousness they shall perish.
>
> As for the truth, it endureth and is always strong; it liveth and conquereth forevermore.
>
> And all the people then shouted and said, Great is Truth and mighty above all things.[4]

Meiklejohn, though he had not the sentiments, had the voice of an evangelical preacher and he made the campus resound with "Women are wicked," and "Great is Truth."

Meiklejohn had certain objections to the St. John's program. It was his opinion, an opinion that went along with his fascination with Kant, that ethics and politics constitute the principal subject matter for a liberal education. From his point of view, St. John's devoted too much time to the study of theology as well as of mathematics and the natural sciences. John Kieffer tells a story of an informal conversation that took place in Buchanan's living room when Meiklejohn was visiting. Buchanan and Meiklejohn were arguing about mathematics, and Buchanan at some point had or seized occasion to repeat what the mathematician Kronecker had said: "God made the integers, and man made the rest [of the real numbers]." Whereupon Meiklejohn, holding up his hand, palm outward, said, "Oh, but there is no God!" Kieffer himself applauded, while Herbert Swartz, a Jewish convert to Roman Catholicism who had come in 1938 from Chicago to join

the faculty, hissed. Among those who shared an allegiance to the St. John's curriculum there was as much disagreement as there is among the authors of great books.

The first time through with the use of great books in the quest for truth brought some changes in Buchanan's plan. There were many books on his original list, especially books that would have been read in the senior year, that were not read by the first new program seniors and were never read. There were some that were read by the first new program seniors and thereafter dropped. Some were dropped after having been read by several generations of students. Of the one hundred nineteen authors in the original list more than fifty have, in the course of time, been removed from the list. Their removal has meant the addition of others. (See Appendix)

These deletions and additions of great books read for the seminar have not very much affected the content or the focus of the seminar discussions for the first three years:

First year: Greek philosophy, poetry, and history.
Second year: The Bible and theology, following some Roman poetry and history and followed by Dante, Chaucer, and Shakespeare;
Third year: Modern philosophy from Descartes to Kant, including modern political philosophy.

In the fourth year seminar, however, there has been a noteworthy change. The first two new program senior classes, although they read a good section of Marx's *Capital,* and although Hegel's *Science of Logic* was on Buchanan's original list, read nothing of Hegel. The third senior class had five seminars on Hegel and six on Marx. No writings of Nietzche or Kierkegaard were read until Buchanan had left St. John's, since he did not consider that these authors had first-rate philosophical minds. Nowadays it is very different. The Hegelian philosophy has become a major focus for seminar discussion for more than half of the senior year, both the Hegelian system in itself and the various ways in which it is opposed and rejected, and yet in some way followed, by Marx, Nietzsche, and Kierkegaard. Whereas in the 1942-43 session, the first time Hegel was read, there were eleven seminars on Hegel and Marx, in the 1980-81 session there were twenty-five seminars on Hegel, Marx, Nietzsche, and Kierkegaard out of a total of forty-two.

During the first few years of the new curriculum, St. John's sponsored monthly radio broadcasts from Station WFBR in Baltimore. These might be talks by Barr or conversations such as one between Taliaferro and Comenetz about the fifth book of Euclid, or they might be fifteen-minute samples of St. John's seminars. They were intended largely for St. John's alumni and were designed to persuade them that the changes being made were something of which they might well approve. Barr insisted that the changes were not revolutionary, or, if revolutionary, were so only as a turning away

from what had been happening to a very large extent in other American colleges where, he maintained, genuine liberal education was being "swayed by sideshow activities, cafeteria courses, and conflicting vocational aims." The St. John's curriculum, he repeated, "is actually old, old as the tradition of liberal education in our Western civilization."

In claiming that the new program was a restoration of a very ancient tradition, he also claimed that it was a restoration of the kind of education that the founders of the American Republic had received and indeed the kind that was intended by the founders of the college when it was chartered in 1784. He liked to quote the words of the charter:

> Whereas institutions for the liberal education of youth in the principles of virtue, knowledge, and useful literature are of the highest benefit to society, in order to train up and perpetuate a succession of able and honest men for discharging the various offices and duties of life, both civil and religious, with usefulness and reputation, and such institutions of learning have accordingly been promoted and encouraged by the wisest and best regulated of States, be it enacted, . . ."

The charter seems to recognize the knowledge or learning acquired through liberal education as something useful, useful for the performance of civil and religious duties. Liberal education, as Barr and Buchanan envisaged it, might indeed be useful for society and religion. But they also saw knowledge and learning as ends to be pursued for their own sake. They certainly did not think that an educational institution should become involved in political action. Buchanan, in a letter of December 16, 1938, to Professor Theodore Brameld of Adelphi College, wrote, "I should like to argue the case for both teachers and students withdrawing from politics for the greater good of everybody."[5] In the same letter, he only somewhat jokingly referred to St. John's as "the awful Ivory Tower."

In one of the broadcasts Barr undertook to remove certain misconceptions of St. John's by stating what the St. John's program is not. It is not, he said, a mere list of books; it is based on great classics studied through carefully organized ways of instruction. It is not just for rich boys who don't have to worry about earning a living; it is to prepare for the business of living as distinguished from the business of earning a living; and the business of living is something that concerns not only the rich. It is not for geniuses; brilliant boys may get more than mediocre boys, but mediocre boys will get more from good reading than from bad. It is not for boys who have been specially prepared for it in some unusual secondary school or through having taken certain unusual courses in such a school. It is not "an interesting experiment in progressive education"; although every good teacher experiments daily in getting out of his students the best he can, St. John's sup-

poses that we know something about what liberal education is, and that we don't have to try it out to see whether it is worthwhile. Finally, it is not a turning away from contemporary America to the dead past of Europe; the past of Europe is our past, and we have to understand our past if we would know ourselves. The great books are those that have "persistently remained contemporary," that is, they have to do with questions that belong to no particular time because they belong to all times.

Another one of these broadcasts was a talk by Buchanan about adult education and what St. John's was doing in adult education. It was his deep conviction that, while the primary service a college performs is the education of youth, it has an obligation to serve the larger community that gives it its financial and moral support. It can do this, he believed, by making it possible for adults to continue learning, for the sake of use or for learning's own sake. He told of the classes that had been offered to adults during the first three years of the new program, classes in such things as writing, cooking, dancing, and Spanish; but also seminars for the discussion of great books. He maintained that practice in leading such seminars for adults was better preparation for the particular St. John's teaching enterprise than Ph.D. training. In 1940 a full-time director of adult education was appointed. This was Olga Plunder, who had been associated with Buchanan in various educational endeavors in New York in the '20s.

In the autumn of 1938 Barr took an action which resulted in the death of fraternities at St. John's. Before he became president, the college had allowed some of its dormitory buildings to be used as fraternity houses. The fraternities paid no rent for these houses. Each member paid the college what he would have paid for an ordinary dormitory room. In some cases there were unoccupied rooms when the fraternity did not have enough members to fill all the rooms in the house. Barr saw no reason why the college should provide fraternity houses in this way, nor did he believe that fraternities were conducive to producing a community of students. He, therefore, announced that at the beginning of the academic session of 1939-40 the college would no longer allow the fraternities to use college buildings. This put an end to the fraternities, for a fraternity isn't much without a fraternity house. The four houses, stripped of their Greek letter fraternity names, were renamed for the four Maryland signers of the Declaration of Independence: Paca, Carroll, Chase and Stone. William Paca was one of the petitioners for the charter of St. John's; the other three signers were all members of the first Board of Visitors and Governors.

A week after taking this action Barr announced that, beginning in September 1939, St. John's would no longer participate in intercollegiate athletics. In giving reasons for the abandonment of intercollegiate athletics Barr stated:

> Intercollegiate athletics involves scheduling games a year or two in advance without reference to the College's internal needs on

Sophomore laboratory session.

the date the contest is played. It involves substituting a spectator psychosis for student participation. It meshes the College in with a semi-professional system in which scores are more important than pleasure and skill.[6]

At the same time he announced that intramural athletics would be greatly expanded and that athletic scholarships would be awarded to young men of athletic prowess who were scholastically able and desirous to pursue the St. John's program of study. These young men would impart their skills and teach athletic prowess to their fellow students.

A poll of the students taken by the *Collegian* showed that the students were overwhelmingly opposed to these two actions on the part of the president, though a number thought that there should be less emphasis on intercollegiate athletics. It seems that new program students objected to these presidential acts as much as the others, though it was especially students who had been around a bit longer who wanted to preserve the memory of St. John's once winning the Olympic championship in lacrosse and the national lacrosse title several times.

More serious was the feeling on the part of the old program students either that they were being got rid of or that they were being neglected. At mid-year during the session when the new program was introduced, twenty-five students were dropped for academic failure. The old programmers spoke of a purge. The dean denied that there was any purge. But the opinion of a purge lingered, since only one of the twenty-five was a new programmer. There was a rumor of a purge the following year which the dean met with a public statement in college meeting in which he gave statistics to show that most of the upper-classmen were in good standing and in no danger of expulsion. But at nearly the same time, the old program students were complaining that the courses being offered them were ridiculously inadequate: the majority were in mathematics and science, and one course only in arts and languages.[7] Many of them thought that Barr and Buchanan had two faces, one for the old programmers and another for the new.

The insistence of Barr and Buchanan on the superiority of the new curriculum no doubt produced some arrogance in the new students. At any rate, the old ones felt it, and as they came to be about equal in number, there was a period described as a period of civil war by Henry Robert, grandson of the author of Robert's *Rules of Order* and one of the first new program students. By the fourth year of the new program the number of old program students was only a dozen or so. Buchanan conducted a seminar for them during the first two of the three terms of their final academic session, and in the third term they were happy to join the new program seminar. Peace and friendship in study and learning characterized the mixed senior class of the session of 1940-41.

Both Barr and Buchanan recognized that, however necessary for the institution of the program their benevolent dictatorship was and however well they worked together, it was highly desirable that the various powers and duties of president, dean, and faculty be defined in a document to be called the college polity which would be accepted by everyone as something of the character of constitutional law for the college community. As early as November 15, 1940, Barr requested the instruction committee "to investigate thoroughly the type of polity that might service the college community best and would be appropriately adapted to and coordinated with the aims of the program."[8]

In November 1943 the faculty elected a committee to draft a polity. George Bingley was made chairman; William A. Darkey, Lewis M. Hammond, William Kyle Smith, and J. Winfree Smith were the other members. The committee went to work at once, and on March 4, 1944, had a tentative polity to submit to the faculty for discussion, criticism, and emendation before any final action was taken. This process, by which nearly the whole faculty participated in formulating the polity, continued almost bimonthly for nearly a year. On January 14, 1945, a draft of the polity, which incorporated the best of all the suggested revisions, was presented for a last informal discussion. A straw vote was taken, and the fifteen faculty members present unanimously approved the draft. (There were then twenty-one members in all.) This, of course, was only an expression of opinion and not a formal action.

At the regular faculty meeting of February 14 this polity was submitted for formal action. William Gorman, who had not been present at the meeting at which the straw vote was taken, and who had not before this either in public or private made any suggestions to the committee, proceeded to read a long statement condemning the polity as submitted. Discussion followed which was cut off short by a motion by Scott Buchanan that the polity be rejected. Gorman had a few followers. Some other members thought that, if Scott Buchanan, whose official acts would henceforth have been largely governed by the polity, didn't want it, it should be defeated. So it was defeated by a vote of ten to five. Buchanan gave no reason for his motion, and no rational explanation has ever appeared.

At the faculty meeting of March 3, 1945, Barr, by presidential fiat, made the rejected polity the official document for the governance of the college, and it continued to be that until well into the presidency of John S. Kieffer, Barr's successor.

The first polity was in many ways simply a regularization of the benevolent dictatorship of Barr and Buchanan. All powers for the "instruction, discipline, and government" of the college were delegated to the president with further power to delegate. To the dean was given the authority

to organize and supervise the program of instruction, and the dean was charged with the responsibility for the governance of the students. He was authorized to appoint an advisory committee of five or more tutors with whom he should consult concerning matters of instruction and to be called the "Instruction Committee." Such a committee was already in existence, set up by Buchanan, and its members appointed by him.

This first polity reflected the strong intention to preserve the program and at the same time to reexamine it with a view to its improvement. The program itself was explicitly made a matter of confidence between the president and the board so that the president would be obliged to resign if the board were to find the program no longer acceptable. Moreover, the dean was required to submit to the faculty biennial statements of educational policy and program to be extensively and searchingly discussed. It was hoped that this requirement, written into the polity, would help to foster a constant renewal of the vision of the ends of education and a constant reexamination of the means to see whether they were serving the ends.

The dean's authority to organize and supervise the program of instruction was to a degree limited. No proposals concerning instruction, no motions concerning instruction, could be made in faculty meeting except by him. Any proposal that he made would become effective unless some faculty member formally registered an objection and held to the objection. In that case the proposal was to be submitted to the vote of the faculty; but before submitting it to vote the dean would declare whether it was a matter of confidence, in which case a negative vote would force the resignation of the dean and the Instruction Committee. If the dean did not think the proposal to be of such importance as to stake his office upon its acceptance or rejection, the matter would be determined by a majority vote of the faculty. This confidence procedure, which has been continued with some modifications up to the present, gave to the dean almost as much power as Buchanan had possessed from the beginning of his incumbency, since it would be extremely unlikely that the faculty would wish to force the resignation of a dean unless there had been a considerable deterioration in his exercise of his office.

There were many times during their first three years at St. John's that Barr and Buchanan wondered whether there would be enough money to keep the college going. They had been in Annapolis hardly a month before they were expressing disappointment at what they considered to be the apathy of the board, and they began to prod the members of the board into action in fund-raising. Buchanan, in a letter to Francis Miller, criticized the board severely for not taking upon themselves the responsibility for obtaining financial support for the college.[9] He thought that, at the time when they had their hands full in inaugurating the new program, Barr should not have to do any money-raising. Barr knew that he couldn't simply leave the money-

raising to the board, but he also could speak of a "general distrust, shared by faculty, students, alumni, and the public, of the board's willingness to put its shoulder to the wheel."[10] These strong words brought some results. A plan was drawn up for paying off the $300,000 mortgage and for dealing with other indebtedness. A financial campaign to be headed by Robert O. Bonnell was to be begun in the autumn.

Several of the board did get to work soliciting funds. Barr, however, was still not satisfied that the board were doing enough, and also thought that Marylanders especially would not be likely to contribute to the college because of lack of confidence in a board that had made so many unwise decisions in the previous decade. In July 1972 he recalled, "I found myself firing the board, which I had sworn not to do."[11] That was probably the fact of the matter, though, of course, he could not legally fire the board. What actually happened was perhaps as illegal and certainly was unusual procedure. At the board meeting of January 10, 1938, a resolution was passed authorizing the president and the chairman of the board to appoint a committee to undertake "The responsibility of securing large contributions from a selected list of prospective donors who might become interested in aiding the college in a substantial manner." At the next meeting in March 1938 that committee, consisting of Barr, Robert Hutchins, Thomas Parran, Colby Chester, and Harold Linder, reported that funds could be secured only if (1) the board were reorganized and (2) the debts of the college readjusted. They recommended that each member of the board resign. The report had been sent out in advance of the meeting, and all the resignations except two, which were tendered later, were in the hands of the president. Thereupon the members who had just resigned voted to elect a committee to proceed immediately to the nomination of members for a "new" board. The committee, of which Barr, Robert Hutchins, Amos Hutchins, and Thomas Parran were members, then submitted its list of nominees, all of whom were elected as board members by those who had resigned and were no longer members of the board. The "new" board so elected contained several members of the "old" board. It was at this same meeting that Robert Hutchins was made chairman of the board. He continued as chairman until the fall of 1939. In spite of heavy duties as president of the University of Chicago, he was rarely absent from board meetings and certainly gave substantial moral support to Barr and Buchanan in their enterprise, besides sending his personal check for $100 regularly every month. Both Buchanan and Barr hoped that Hutchins would, at some point, leave Chicago and become president of St. John's. Buchanan, in his letter to Francis Miller in July of 1937 had said, "We are seriously waiting for the time when Bob Hutchins can come and do the administrative duties for us and with us."[12] Barr himself, as he has said repeatedly, never wanted to be a college presi-

dent. His letters to Hutchins in 1937 and 1938 contain frequent urgings to come to St. John's. On September 26, 1938 he wrote:

> I am perfectly aware of all the difficulties, but I regard it as fundamentally an absurdity that you should not be here instead of there. This is not to be construed as a complaint, much less a cry of despair, but as a candid comment on the sort of thing that is going on here. I wish to God you were involved with it daily, immediately, and locally.[13]

A month later he wrote more extensively on the same subject to Mortimer Adler, who was himself sympathetic to the idea of Hutchins's becoming president of St. John's:

> When I left Chicago, I hoped that by some miracle Bob might eventually take over. Frankly, it was a queer kind of hope, in view of the sacrifice, at least on the surface, which this would impose on Bob. I know that Bob would have to be very large-sized and a very clear-headed man to make such a move . . . I became convinced before leaving Chicago that Bob was both these things . . .
> It seems to me that since I left Chicago, two things have been happening. First, I judge from Bob's talk with me that Chicago is becoming less and less real. I do not feel that Bob wasted his time going there. Chicago furnished him with a unique sounding board and he used this sounding-board to unique advantage. But I fear that he has now said all that has to be said and that further progress lies only in the direction of doing. Bob talks about not being a scholar or a teacher but an administrator. . . . Unfortunately I judge he's less and less sure that, in terms of the peculiar contribution he should be making to American education, Chicago is worth administering. On the other hand, while the emptiness of Chicago has been becoming increasingly obvious to Bob, the St. John's Program has become increasingly what Bob has fought for. Since St. John's is the only embodiment in America of the ideal liberal undergraduate education that Bob has fought for, his residence in Chicago appears increasingly perverse and wasteful to those who know the facts.[14]

CHAPTER 5

Criticism from Outside and Inside and Effect of World War II

Hutchins, Adler, and Barr were not simply advocates of a different kind of college education from what was to be found in American colleges and universities generally. They were constantly attacking college education in institutions other than St. John's. Barr in a public address would say such things as: "Modern college education is being conducted in a new tower of Babel staffed by professors often proud of their own ignorance, its corridors crammed with bewildered students learning a hodgepodge of useless skills and becoming increasingly unintelligible to one another and to the world they face." Hutchins and Barr were devastatingly witty, and this made their attacks all the more effective and provocative. Hutchins and Adler tended to blame John Dewey and his followers for much that they considered wrong with American college education.

It was understandable, then, that there were various counterattacks and especially from the followers of Dewey. Dewey himself in August 1944 published an article in *Fortune* called "A Challenge to Liberal Thought." The article did not refer by name to any of the challengers except Robert Hutchins. It did mention Hutchins's "theological fellow travelers." It did not mention St. John's, but it was generally taken to be directed at St. John's because of such sentences as: "The idea that an adequate education can be obtained by means of a miscellaneous assortment of a hundred books, more or less, is laughable when viewed practically."[1] Dewey concluded from Hutchins's claim that human nature is everywhere and always the same that Hutchins must also think that the principles governing human conduct are unchangeable, that they are to be found not by experimental inquiry or direct observation, but in books. He saw this partly as a reversion to antiquity but even more as a reversion to what he considered to be the antiscientific dogmatism of the Middlge Ages. Dewey himself was, of course, particularly concerned that education should follow the way of experiment and observation as much in the study of man and society as in the study of nonhuman things. He saw this way as closely linked with freedom of inquiry

made possible by democracy and with the technological control of nature. Hutchins and his friends were, in his opinion, antiscientific, antidemocratic dogmatists, mindful only of the past and oblivious to the present.

In the issue of *Fortune* for January 1945 Alexander Meiklejohn had "A Reply to John Dewey." Meiklejohn quite naturally supposed that Dewey was attacking the St. John's curriculum, and his reply was largely a defense of that curriculum.

Against the charge that the St. John's way of studying the past led to dogmatism, to the acceptance of some set of beliefs held by somebody in the past, he pointed out that in reading and discussing the great books a St. John's student meets not just one set of beliefs, but many conflicting sets; that he "will find Protagoras at war with Plato, Kant at war with Hume, Rousseau at war with Locke, Veblen at war with Adam Smith, and he must try to understand both sides of these controversies."[2] To the charge that reading a miscellaneous collection of great books in the four college years is laughable as a way of education, when viewed practically, he replied that, for all the startling audacity of having college students read many such very difficult books, the studying of these books was not irresponsibily done, being subject through careful discussion to guidance, correction, and criticism. Against the charge that St. John's ignores the way of experimental inquiry and observation, he pointed out that every student at St. John's was required to devote half of his course of study to the learning of science and of mathematics as the 'language' upon which scientific achievement depends.

In regard to this disagreement between Dewey and Meiklejohn, it should be noted that they both assumed that the St. John's kind of education involved an interest in the past as such. That was, and still is, incorrect. Teachers and students have no interest in studying the past as past. They have an interest in reading certain books that were written in the past because those books raise important perennial questions, questions which are always live and present questions if we let our thought get hold of them. Moreover, St. John's was and is perhaps more radical than either Dewey or Meiklejohn was. For Dewey, while acknowledging that a study of the past is necessary for understanding the present, was quite sure that modern thought represents a tremendous gain over ancient and medieval thought. Meiklejohn, though quite clear about controversy between such thinkers as Hume and Kant, nonetheless thought and supposed it to be a basic postulate of St. John's that "from the time of the Greeks until the present the knowledge and wisdom of men have been growing." Actually, at St. John's it would be a question whether there has been such growth, a question not so easily answered if by wisdom is meant the wisdom about the whole of things. While one could hardly deny that there has been a tremendous growth of 'knowledge' in the modern natural sciences, of which St. John's tries to take sufficient cognizance, it is not easy to decide whether Plato or Hegel were closer to the knowledge of the whole of things.

Dewey's response to Meiklejohn was a letter to *Fortune* in which he said that he had not been referring to St. John's at all in his "A Challenge to Liberal Thought."

> The philosophy I criticized [he wrote] is so current and so much more influential than is the work of St. John's, there are only a few sentences in my article even indirectly referring to St. John's. Rightly or wrongly, I had not supposed that the program and work of St. John's was of such importance as to justify my use of the pages of *Fortune* in extended criticism of it, especially as a number of effective criticisms of it had already been made.[3]

The criticisms to which he was referring were principally those of Sidney Hook, which had appeared in *The New Leader* of May 26, 1944, and June 3, 1944, and were later included in a book entitled *Education for Modern Man* under the title, "A Critical Appraisal of the St. John's College Curriculum." Some of Hook's criticisms were the same that Dewey had made of Hutchins and Hutchins's "fellow travelers." He claimed that the people at St. John's thought that man has an essential unchangeable nature and that the unchangeable truth about man's nature and about all things can be learned because it is written down in ancient and medieval books, that to possess these truths all one has to do is to read those books. He mentioned that it was the hidden assumption in the philosophy underlying St. John's that "the true answers to our problems can be found by assaying the heritage of antiquity and the Middle Ages."[4] He recognized that in studying books written in ancient Greece the St. John's people were not seeking to know Greek man but to know about human nature, but he seemed to think that what one learns directly from a Greek book is only something about Greek man. He raised the question others have raised through the years, of why there are no Chinese or Hindu books in the St. John's list, why, granted that the reading of ancient literature develops the imagination, the reading of ancient oriental literature might not produce an imaginative sympathy with the problems and experience of those Eastern people with whom we have to deal and will have to deal. He attacked what he considered to be the St. John's doctrine that there is "transfer of learning." Presumably he was referring, for example, to the assumption that in studying the grammar of one language one can learn certain things that appear universally in language, the knowledge of which will be profitable in learning any language and in learning how language may be a means of inquiry or may convey truth about things. He also attacked the view that a good way to learn mathematics and science is through the reading of classical works in those areas, and he invoked the formidable names of Richard Courant, Bertrand Russell, and Albert Einstein in support of his attack, all of whom in letters which he quoted supposed that what was in question was a study

of the historical development of mathematics and science rather than an understanding of what is fundamental in them through sharing and exploring the thought of the original discoverers. Those responsible for the St. John's curriculum never supposed that it would always be the case that the original discoverer of a science or a scientific theory would make a more intelligible presentation of it than someone else. That it is usually the case is not something known *a priori,* but is a matter of the long experience of both ways of presentation.

Some of Sidney Hook's criticisms were justified. Barr's harsh judgments of other colleges went too far. Barr had no doubt made exaggerated claims when he said that the St. John's students were going to read every one of the books on the list in its entirety. It was certainly debatable whether the whole St. John's curriculum were suitable, as Barr maintained, for all students of college age. It was certainly conceivable that a college student might learn as much from analyzing a bad book such as Hitler's *Mein Kampf* as from reading a good or a great book. All of these were points that Hook made. But on the whole his "critical appraisal" was based on misconceptions. One reason that he had these misconceptions was that he assumed that anything Hutchins or Adler said St. John's would endorse. This illusion on his part was understandable in view of Hutchins's close connection with the college, first as a member, and then as chairman, of the board, and also in view of Adler's position as lecturer at the college and his constant support of it in public utterances. Hook referred to Adler both as Hutchins's mentor and as the "mentor of the St. John's educators."[5]

Hook should nonetheless have known better, since before writing his articles for the *New Leader* he had had several letters from Buchanan that attempted to limit and define their differences. These letters indeed affirmed "the rational scientific nature" of metaphysics, politics, and religion. He could hardly expect Hook to agree that metaphysics and religion were scientific. At the same time, he explicitly refused to deny "the rational scientific nature" of social studies, which he knew Hook would strongly affirm. He vigorously resisted the charge of indoctrination, insisting that he would "defend the freedom of the intellect and the will in considering them [the studies mentioned, especially metaphysics and theology] in such a way as to show that indoctrination in them is impossible."[6] Later on he wrote urging Hook to come to the college and lecture; he mentioned several possible topics: "Karl Marx," "The St. John's Brand of 'Indoctrination' " (as Hook saw it), "The Scientific Method, Intelligence and Society."[7] He suggested that such a lecture would be of great aid in the lively controversies that had been going on within the college now that there were faculty and students who had read the whole list of books, were caught up in the quarrel between the ancients and the moderns, and had engaged in considerable debate about Marx.

It was not possible for Hook to visit St. John's at that time, and by the

time he published the *New Leader* articles the character of the exchange of correspondence that he had with Buchanan made the visit increasingly unlikely. It became clearer and clearer that his principal target was Adler, but Hook could never come to terms with Buchanan as long as Buchanan failed to repudiate publicly those statements or positions of Adler with which Buchanan disagreed. On January 26, 1943, Hook wrote to Buchanan:

> I am glad to learn that you haven't joined the neo-Thomist "gang." I don't recall using the word, but now that you have used it I think it quite apt. A "gang" is a group of people who are unalterably committed to a vested interest or doctrine, even if truth, honor, and justice be elsewhere. . . . A large number of people, however, believe, apparently on insufficient evidence, that doctrinally you are approaching the neo-Thomists more closely than one would expect on the basis of your personal outlook and better knowledge of your earlier philosophical position. As the leading spirit of an important educational enterprise I think you should be concerned about the generality of this impression. I am taking the liberty of suggesting that it would be helpful if you found an opportunity to state publicly what you thought about the doctrine of neo-Thomism from its sacred theology to its educational philosophy.[8]

In spite of disagreements with Adler, Buchanan could not repudiate him in any way that would be satisfactory to Hook. With his view that metaphysics and theology, even if not wholly identical with any metaphysics and theology of the past, were the sciences that would give unity to all knowledge, Buchanan could not well repudiate the neo-Thomists in a way that would be satisfactory to Hook.

After the *New Leader* articles severely critical of Barr as well as of Adler, the exchange between Hook and Buchanan became more and more acrimonious. Buchanan kept inviting Hook to come to St. John's, spend a while, and see for himself. Hook refused to come on the ground that, if he came and found that things were just as he expected, Buchanan would discover one reason after another to explain why he had not been able to put his ideas into execution.

Buchanan did not in any of his letters to Hook reply to the question about oriental classics. His position on the subject was, however, made clear in a reply that he wrote in the spring of 1940 to a letter that made a plea for the inclusion of such classics in the list of great books:

> Four years [he wrote] is a short time for reading the books we already have on the list. If I did not think people would go on

gradually studying the books these lead to I should think we were a complete fake. We are doing the first reading of the few books which will initiate us to the study of all the things we should know, including other books. I think the great books of the Orient are included in that perspective.[9]

Clearly, Chinese and Hindu books were not in principle excluded from the St. John's curriculum.

The students at St. John's have, on the whole, not been critical of the conception and plan of the curriculum. Perhaps in many cases their decision to attend St. John's rather than some other college has meant an acceptance of that conception and that plan. Most of the students' criticism has been to the effect that the college, while being right and quite articulate about its aims, did not in performance live up to its aims. Not much of this criticism was expressed until the program had been in operation for a few years. Many of the first new programmers within a very short time began to look back on their student days as a "golden age."

The golden age probably never existed. There was indeed a certain excitement among the first new programmers which arose not simply because significant learning is exciting but also because of their belonging to a group who were engaged not in an experiment, but in something new in relation to the conventionalities of other colleges.

One record of student commentary and criticism was the college yearbook, the student editors of which, during the Barr-Buchanan era, were exceptionally intelligent and perceptive. The *Nineteen Forty Yearbook* mentions what are called "difficulties" encountered in the first year of the program, difficulties that were said to have been overcome or to be in the process of being overcome. The difficulties seem to have been caused by the demands on the student's time that went beyond those of the officially announced curriculum. There were lectures for all students twice a week, each of which lasted from two to two and one-half hours. There were, in addition, supplementary lectures on Platonic dialogues. There was a special tutorial for practice in writing in addition to the language tutorial. To discuss the dialogues of Plato in seminar fashion was no doubt a more Socratic way of getting into them than by listening to lectures. In any case, the supplementary lectures were soon eliminated, practice in writing was assigned to the language tutorial, and the number of lectures reduced to one a week with an hour and a half as the time limit. "The greatest difficulty this class [the first new program class] has met so far in connection with the curriculum," the *Nineteen Forty Yearbook* reported, "has been the laboratory. After the class had roamed aimlessly for a year or so in its lab work a method of instruction has been developed that runs much more smoothly and is better correlated with the rest of the Program."[10]

Alfred Eisenstaedt/Life Magazine

James S. Martin delivers lecture.

The entry of the United States into World War II brought many changes in the college. In October 1939 the *St. John's Collegian* took a poll among the students to get their opinion about United States policy in relation to the war which had already begun in Europe. Eighty-one students responded to the five questions that were asked. The questions and the results of the poll were as follows:[11]

1. Should the United States give immediate armed support to the European democracies?

Yes	No	No opinion
8	72	1

2. Should this country assist England and France by filling, as far as possible, their demands for munitions and commodities such as food, raw materials, and manufactured goods?

Yes	No	No opinion
34	42	5

3. Should America pursue a policy of strict isolationism concerning European affairs?

Yes	No	No opinion
38	41	2

4. Do you think Britain and France should attempt to make peace with Germany at this stage of the war?

Yes	No	No opinion
21	55	5

5. In case of this country's engaging in the present war in Europe, would you volunteer before a draft were effected?

Yes	No	No opinion
27	55	4

In over a hundred colleges throughout the country similar polls were taken and with similar results. At that time American college students were strongly opposed to sending American troops to support England and France but a larger percentage (42 per cent) than was the case at St. John's were willing to volunteer if England and France were in danger of defeat.

Student opinion at St. John's seems to have changed by the time of the attack on Pearl Harbor in December 1941. When the news of Pearl Harbor came, there was, according to the *Nineteen Forty Yearbook,* much talk among the students about enlistment. A college meeting was called the day after and the students expected Barr and Buchanan to plead with them to stay at least until June 1942. Barr did not plead with them to stay. Having made the point that only a few ever take part in what the young might consider the romantic adventures of war, he suggested a definite choice either to enlist or to stay and work at studies. He even suggested that it might be their duty to stay; he believed that it was of the utmost importance that good thinking about war and peace should go on while the country was at war

and that colleges, especially St. John's College, should not close, but stay open and think about war and peace. Buchanan at the same college meeting spoke of the problems that would arise in the relation of the college to the townspeople who, as the country became more and more involved in the war, would judge and condemn those young men who were studying God knows what when they ought to be fighting in defense of their country. The editor of the yearbook, John Louis Hedeman, ended his account of this meeting with the report that "for the most part, students, thinking things over, found that a year or even two or three in the army did not appeal to them and went back to their seminars to discuss the same problems in the light of ages past."[12]

The college administration took various steps to prepare the students in what they thought might be useful in the war. There was a three-hour course once a week in radio. There was a course in navigation. Franz Plunder, a sculptor and boat-builder, who also possessed many other skills, taught a group of about sixty persons the intricacies of the gasoline engine, for, as the *Nineteen Forty-Two Yearbook* put it, "no one knew which St. Johnnie might be stranded in a tank somewhere on the battlefront, where there would be no hardware store and mechanics for him to turn to."[13] The press poked a certain amount of fun at the "great books" college for this course in the gasoline engine. Actually the course was in line with Buchanan's view that there is a training of the intellect that happens in the learning and practice of the manual arts as well as the liberal arts. Also, Buchanan knew that one learns quite a bit of physics if one acquires a full understanding of all the transformations of energy that take place in the internal combustion engine.

Whether these courses were in fact useful to many of the students when later they were in military service is doubtful. But at the time they helped them to feel that they were not just engaged in talk about the war but were doing something. In spite of the talk that went on in meetings to discuss the war, and in spite of the activities just mentioned, the war did not have a great impact upon the college during the session of 1941-42. Many students, through joining the reserves, were able to finish the year. All students, not just the reservists, were required to take part in military drill, which all accepted, though some found it irksome. It was in the following session that the war really began to have a big effect. At the beginning of that session there were 173 students enrolled. By the end of the year there were fewer than a hundred. When the next session began, there were only forty-two in the three upper classes. Only seven of the ninety-three in the *"Life* class" remained to receive degrees in 1944. Not only were students leaving in droves for military service, but faculty were leaving too, among them some who had contributed most to get the program established and to make it go: George Comenetz, Catesby Taliaferro, John Neustadt, and Raymond

Wilburn. There were also very promising newcomers on the faculty who had hardly been at the college a year before having to leave for military service or for some employment related to the war effort.

The president and the dean thought that it would be fitting to mark with a ceremony the departure of students for the war. During the 1942-43 session there were two occasions when a solemn ceremony was held in the college's Great Hall, and all those leaving for the war took the Ephebic oath administered by Barr. This oath was once taken by Athenian youth as they were going off to war:

> I will not disgrace the name of my country and I will not desert my comrades in the ranks. By myself and with my fellows I will defend what is sacred, whether private or public. I will hand on my country not lessened but greater and nobler than it was handed down to me. I will hearken diligently to those duly charged with judging, and I will obey the established laws and whatever others the people with common consent establish. And if anyone attempts to overthrow the laws, or not obey them, I will not stand idly by but by myself and with all my comrades I will defend the law. And I will honor the religion of my fathers. The gods be witness of these things.[14]

There were some who wondered how American youth could honor the religion of their fathers and at the same time call upon the Greek gods to witness their oath. But everyone felt the seriousness of the occasion. Some of the young men who took the oath were to give their lives in combat. Many were to follow Barr's admonition, given on that occasion, not to forget in the midst of all the irrationality of war that there is still such a thing as human reason. Many, too, would return when the war was over.

Obviously, the college had to take some drastic steps if it were not to close its doors. It was decided to admit as freshmen at the beginning of every term fifteen-year-olds who had not finished high school,[15] and also to add a summer term to the three terms already current. In this way a fifteen-year-old could complete his college course in three years and do so before being subject to the draft. With the admission of freshmen in June and September 1943 the total enrollment went up to 138, and it never again fell as low as it did in the spring of 1943. In the fall of 1946, when the accelerated schedule had already been abandoned, the return of veterans shot the enrollment up to 253.

The yearbooks for 1944 and for 1945-46, edited by Robert Campbell and Eugene Thaw, reflect a considerable amount of self-criticism on the part of students and also criticism of the college. The loss of such a large portion of the students in 1942-43 was very depressing for those who re-

mained, who, if they were not wondering when they themselves might have to leave, were agonizingly asking themselves whether staying in college and studying were the best thing to be doing when their friends were engaged in a war, the outcome of which was so important for human life on this planet. "We neglected our studies," Campbell wrote in the *Nineteen Forty-four Yearbook,* "and sought diversion. . . . We became adept and ingenious at excusing our own vices and our facility in this respect usually manifested itself in criticism, not of the Program itself (for we knew too well its necessity, goodness, and consequences) but of the way in which it was being applied."[16] The students do not seem to have shared Buchanan's opinion that the books are the teachers and that the faculty are decidedly of minor importance. The loss not only of some of the best students, but also of outstanding faculty was considered a serious injury to successful study within the program. Said Campbell,

> The advent of war, although unable to affect the Program, certainly introduced deficiencies into the teaching of it. A good faculty is absolutely essential to good participation in the program by the student body. It may be argued that the books, are, after all, the teachers, and that the student learns from them rather than from the faculty, the latter being only the means leading the students to the end, but from this it would be difficult to conclude that the quality of the means is unimportant.[17]

He found the faculty who had come to replace those who had left definitely inferior.

Also the great number of young freshmen and the small number of upperclassmen, so Campbell thought, destroyed the learning community as a community, even if individually some students were doing better work than they had done before. The juniors and seniors, instead of communicating to the freshmen customs and habits conducive to the kind of study most suitable for success within the program, retired into small groups and left the freshmen to produce, or not to produce, their own traditions.

"The Iron Age" was the title given to the next yearbook, edited by Eugene Thaw, which was a two-year book since the drafting of two editors into military service had prevented the production of a yearbook in 1945. The title indicated that the two years covered were being thought of as a period of decline from an earlier 'golden age', but also along with the dedication to Virgil it indicated a hope for a golden age to come. The yearbook spoke of a "trend of decline" in all sections of the program except the formal lectures. It complained of student lethargy and of inadequate preparation for tutorials with the result that much routine work which should have been done outside of class had to be done in class. The claim was made that the

seminars had suffered as a consequence. The tutorials were called the "mainstay of the program" as the place for the acquisition of skills to be exhibited and tested in the seminar. "The seminar," it was said, "is the finished product of the program, accomplished and consummate, however, only to the degree of success in tutorial."[18]

In the fall of 1945 there was a change in schedule from five one-hour tutorial classes a week to three classes with normal length of an hour-and-a-half. This was thought to have produced improvement in the quality of the tutorials. But it was set down as a disadvantage that the new scheduling had made it impossible for a student to attend a language or mathematics tutorial other than the one to which he had been assigned. The mere fact that a student might want to attend another such class with the expectation of getting a better understanding than he had got in his assigned class pointed to the strong student opinion that it mattered very much that the tutors were unequal in teaching ability and in their grasp of what they were teaching.

As Campbell had done in the *Nineteen Forty-four Yearbook,* Thaw made a plea for a place for the fine arts within the curriculum. Music as a fine art has, since the time of Barr and Buchanan, had some place in the curriculum. Concerts have been given on certain Friday evenings instead of lectures. Herbert Swartz in 1938, Elliott Carter in 1940, and Nicholas Nabokov in 1941 were all added to the Faculty in large part because of their musical knowledge which, it was expected, would enable them to suggest how music as a fine art might fit into the curriculum and also to sponsor and supervise music as an extracurricular activity. None of them remained very long and little came of their efforts. When Carter and Nabokov were at the college there were seminars on musical compositions, but the musicians were at odds with Buchanan, who thought that one should study the scores without listening to and without ever having listened to the sounds represented by the staves with their whole notes, half notes and quarter-notes, etc., and without even knowing that those marks might refer to sounds.

In August 1937 Buchanan had written on the subject of the college and the fine arts to an inquirer:

> In our study of liberal college education, we have been forced to consider the bookish classics as the basic medium of our teaching. There is a sense in which great books are works of fine art; on the other hand, we realize very vividly that we are ignoring, or seeming to ignore, the classics in the fine arts proper. When we have consolidated our program, we shall turn very definitely to the problem of teaching the fine arts as well as the liberal arts. In the meantime we shall proceed tentatively with extracurricular activities in the fine arts.[19]

Buchanan had a theory about the fine arts, namely that at the Renaissance they had become substitutes for the sacraments. He no doubt would have liked to have St. John's discover the right way of combining divine arts, liberal arts, fine arts, and manual arts. During the Barr-Buchanan era, however, little was done to encourage the study of works of fine art besides musical works. Edgar Wind of the Warburg Institute gave some excellent lectures on the School of Athens, the frescoes of the Sistine ceiling, and Hogarth, but that was about all. When later Jacob Klein became dean, he even called in question the meaningfulness of the term "fine arts" as applied in common to music and the visual arts. Herbert Swartz, in a radio talk in 1939, explaining the place of music in a liberal arts college program, argued that what music, painting, and sculpture have in common is that they are *end* arts rather than useful arts, arts the products of which are to be understood and enjoyed for their own sake rather than arts the products of which are to be used. In any case, whether works of music, painting, and sculpture are all of the same kind or not, Eugene Thaw in the *Nineteen Forty-five — Forty-six Yearbook* wrote convincingly, "It seems not too much to ask an undergraduate college concerned with producing well-educated men to take notice of Michelangelo and Pheidias."[20]

CHAPTER 6

The Fight with the Navy in Wartime and the Departure of Barr and Buchanan

This is a strange, and perhaps incomprehensible, story. The struggle over the possible acquisition by the Navy of the St. John's campus had three distinct episodes. Its outcome was favorable to St. John's in the judgment of nearly everyone except Barr and Buchanan, whose departure shortly thereafter astonished nearly everyone.

The first of these episodes began in 1940. It was announced to the faculty in September of that year that there was a rumor that the United States Naval Academy, whose grounds are separated from the St. John's campus only by a street,[1] wished to acquire the campus. Admiral Wilson Brown, then Superintendent of the Naval Academy, and Stringfellow Barr, who had very amicable relations with each other, went together to Washington on October first to appear before the Senate Appropriations Committee who were considering the question of the acquisition of the campus by the Navy for the expansion of the Academy. An exchange of correspondence between Barr and Brown occurred shortly after that . Barr wrote, "It seems to me desirable that I should repeat to you in writing what I then stated to the committee. You will recall that I was asked by Senator Byrnes [James Byrnes, later Secretary of State] what would be my attitude as President of St. John's College towards a proposal by the Navy Department to purchase the College in order to expand the present facilities of the Naval Academy. You will also doubtless recall my reply that as President of the College I would urgently recommend to the trustees that they reject such a proposal unless it could be clearly demonstrated that the exigencies of the national defense program required the Naval Academy to secure our property rather than other available land."[2]

Shortly after that the Secretary of the Navy, Frank Knox, stated that the Navy would make no attempt to take the St. John's campus provided that St. John's agree to two conditions laid down by President Franklin Roosevelt: (1) that the college not dispose of her property without first noti-

fying the Navy and giving the Navy a chance to purchase it; (2) that the land not be used for any other purpose than that of the college and that no other than college buildings be erected upon it. Agreement on the second condition put an end to an attempt by the Annapolis Housing Authority to take by condemnation one and a third acres of the campus as a site for low cost housing for white people of moderate income. Barr was only too glad to assent to these conditions and by January 31, 1941, he was able to report to the St. John's board that "the question of the Naval Academy's acquiring the property of the College was now definitely settled."[3]

The second episode was very brief. It occurred in July 1942 when the United States was already at war, and the Navy was faced with the necessity of expanding its facilities for the training of officers. On July 15, Barr wrote to Knox reminding him of positions taken by St. John's and the Navy when Wilson Brown had been Superintendent of the Academy, and reporting that an aide to the then superintendent had appeared on the campus to look it over to see whether it could be used as an indoctrination school for Naval Reserve officers. He went on to say, "It is most doubtful whether the College could survive transplanting," but continued, "I am certain you will not construe this letter as an objection to the Navy's defense [presumably of the country]." The secretary replied that such surveys as the aide was making were being made at institutions in many places and that there was no specific proposal about the St. John's campus.[4]

The third episode, the dramatic culmination, began early in 1945. On February 28 of that year, Barr reported to the board as follows:

> Because of persistent and increasing rumors that the Navy Department is about to seize St. John's College or that the State of Maryland might 'acquire' the College (possibly in order later to 'decide' to hand it over to the Navy Department) I ought to report to you what facts I possess.
>
> On February 13, 1945, Delegate Bertram L. Boone (D. 5th, Baltimore) introduced a bill in the Maryland House of Delegates calling for appointment of a commission to examine the possibility of the State's taking over St. John's. In presenting the bill, Mr. Boone announced, 'The thing is going to pot.'
>
> The next day I stated in the press that 'St. John's College is not for sale,' and a 'spokesman' for the Navy Department said, 'The Navy has no present plans for the acquisition of St. John's College.'
>
> Meanwhile, Mrs. Douglas Howard, widow of Captain Howard, once Dean of St. John's College, had written Admiral Ernest King, who is an intimate friend of hers, urging that the

Navy Department disassociate itself from the Navy-Realtor clique, a clique that has now resorted to defamation of the College in order to squeeze it out of town. Mrs. Howard showed me Ernie's reply which was to the effect that the rumor has substantial basis in fact, that the Academy was to be approximately double its size and that the most available land for this expansion was our campus and the three blocks of residence property between the Academy and King George St. Admiral King stated that the matter would be decided by the President at the end of this month. I have since learned that Admiral Wilson Brown, formerly Superintendent of the Academy and most friendly to the College, now once more Naval Aide to the President, has several times blocked seizure.

I am personally disinclined to pull wires to prevent seizure. The Navy, it should be reported, feels more threatened than we do — by the California delegation in Congress, which is working to get a part of their establishment here moved to the Coast. This fact is known to the business element of Annapolis, who therefore feel the College is standing between them and their bread and butter. The College's relations with the town have, therefore, never been more painful during my administration.[5]

On March 9, James V. Forrestal, Secretary of the Navy, and Admiral Chester Nimitz had lunch with President Roosevelt and, as Forrestal reports in his Diary:[6]

I told him [Roosevelt] of Senator Tydings' inquiry regarding St. John's College. He said he thought it was desirable to acquire the St. John's grounds and buildings but would like to see the buildings preserved. I told him I shared his feeling and reported Admiral King's suggestion that we grasp the nettle firmly and go across the river to acquire land for expansion of the Academy. The general conclusion was:
   a. Acquire St. John's
   b. Keep the buildings and grounds intact
   c. Proceed with acquisition of land across the river for further additions to the Academy.

This entry in Forrestal's diary supports Admiral King's statement to Mrs. Howard that the rumor had "substantial basis in fact." No one connected with St. John's knew of this meeting with Roosevelt, but, because the persistent rumor did appear to have a basis in fact, the Board, no doubt with

the approval, if not under the prompting of Barr and Buchanan, on April 21, 1945, formulated the following statement of policy to be sent to Secretary Forrestal:

> 1. The present uncertainty, aggravated by irresponsible rumors of imminent condemnation of the College's property, is harmful to the morale of the College, to its relations with the Annapolis community, and to the College Administration's ability to exercise its function wisely or to plan intelligently for future building now in prospect. An immediate understanding with the Navy Department is accordingly imperative.
>
> 2. This Board is entrusted with and proposes to fulfill the continuing responsibility of carrying on vigorously the function of the College, and cannot deal with its property as mere real estate and buildings. The Board believes that this function could be carried on elsewhere, in spite of obvious problems and difficulties, if an adequate site and the means of acquiring it could be made available. The Board, however, feels that it cannot properly or intelligently consider removing the College from its historic site in Annapolis unless the Navy Department formally represents to the Board that acquisition of the College property is required in the national interest. The Board, obviously, could not undertake to pass judgement on the decision of the Navy Department. Nor does the Board propose to interpose any objection to such acquisition, provided that the arrangements permit the Board, in its judgment, to continue to carry on the work of the College, and to discharge its legal and moral obligations to its college community, including faculty, students, alumni, the benefactors, creditors, and the State of Maryland.
>
> 3. The Board respectfully records its conviction that the Navy Department has a genuine responsibility in the premises to dispose of the present damaging impasse by plainly advising the Board at this time whether or not it now requires the College property for the national welfare; and furthermore, whether or not present plans for the future will require it. [Statement of Policy, St. John's College Archives.]

This statement of policy was the crucial document in the whole affair. Whereas Barr's letter to Knox four years earlier had said, "It's doubtful whether the College could survive transplanting" this statement says "The Board believes this function [the function of educating] could be carried on elsewhere in spite of obvious problems and difficulties, if an adequate site and the means of acquiring it could be made available." Also, whereas in 1940 Barr had said that he would recommend that the trustees reject the

proposal for acquisition unless it could be *clearly demonstrated* that the exigencies of the national defense program required the Naval Academy to secure the College property, etc., this statement makes no mention of clear demonstration but asks that the Navy Department *formally represent* to the board that "acquisition of the College property is required in the national interest." It goes on to say that the board "could not undertake to pass judgment on the decision of the Navy Department," that the board does not "propose to interpose any objection to such acquisition whether by formal condemnation or negotiation, provided that the arrangements permit the board, in its judgment, to continue to carry on the work of the College," etc.

The admirals and the Secretary of the Navy little knew what this statement of policy was going to get them into. They understood it as tantamount to an offer. That this was the Navy's interpretation is clear from the subsequent testimony of Admiral Moreell, Chief of the Bureau of Yards and Docks, before the Senate Naval Affairs Committee. Admiral Moreell stated, "The acquisition of the adjoining property [the St. John's campus] has been under consideration for a number of years, but the Department has not advanced this project due to the reluctance of the board of governors and visitors of the college to dispose of this property. The college authorities, however, have recently expressed a willingness to dispose of the property to the Navy Department in the event that it is needed in connection with the Naval Academy."[7] It certainly appeared to the admirals that St. John's was ready to let the Navy have the campus provided the Navy did no more than declare the acquisition necessary in the national interest and provided that the college receive sufficient compensation to enable it to continue elsewhere as the distinguished liberal arts college it had become.

The board's action, interpreted as it was by the Navy, precipitated the Navy's final and most serious attempt to acquire the St. John's campus. On April 27, 1945, Secretary Forrestal wrote to Thomas Parran, chairman of the St. John's board and at that time Surgeon General of the United States: "It now appears that the expansion of the Naval Academy will require the acquisition of the present property belonging to St. John's College." But he had not declared that the acquisition was necessary in the national interest. On May 5 Dr. Parran, in a letter to Secretary Forrestal, inquired when the Navy would acquire the campus since plans for the removal of the college would require more definite knowledge. A month later Forrestal replied that negotiations would begin immediately.[8] The Naval Affairs committees of the Senate and the House still had to approve the acquisition, but the Secretary of the Navy seems to have had little doubt that they would. On May 7 Buchanan wrote to Robert Hutchins:

> Perhaps you ought to know my opinion of certain events here. You will have seen our communication with James Forrestal. You may not have heard the reply. It is that the expansion of

the Naval Academy will require the acquisition of the St. John's campus. Action waits on Congressional appropriation. What had appeared in prospect as a desirable event is, because of numerous circumstances, becoming a crisis. Where do we go and how? Do we go or not?[9]

Hutchins replied, "You really say something when you say the Naval Academy requires the campus and is merely waiting for an appropriation. This sounds to me like an Opportunity."[10]

What was the event desirable in prospect? Was it the acquisition of the campus by the Navy? And was the "Opportunity" that of moving the St. John's program from a place where, as Buchanan thought, the Navy was always making it difficult to pursue the program? A letter of about the same time from Buchanan to Senator Wayne Morse claimed that the Naval Academy dominated Annapolis commercially, was pandered to by the city and county governments, and that the state government paid more attention to the Navy than to the public welfare.[11] He clearly thought that the mere presence of the Navy was damaging not only to the college, but to the town and to the state and to the citizens of the town and of the state.

As early as June 1944 he had written in a letter to his son Douglas,

> Winkie and I have today been wondering again how to extricate the program from this place. It is now quite clear that the academy is what has kept this poor little college sick for almost a century. We can't see how we move alive but we can see that we ought to have done so a year ago last January when we had to decide whether we would suspend operations or take youngsters. We should have suspended; a great deal of damage to the idea itself has resulted from our noble decision to carry on.

A year later he wrote, "The Navy has turned the town into a little Fascist community governed by greed and fear."

What caused the event desirable in prospect to become a crisis? For one thing, alumni tend not to think of the college they have attended as an invisible chartered entity which might exist on other land and in other buildings than those in which they used to eat, sleep, study, and learn. So it was with St. John's alumni. The president of the Alumni Association, William Lentz, a Baltimore lawyer, wrote Senator Radcliffe on behalf of the association, protesting the annexation of the campus by the Academy. He stated that the alumni "feel that it is detrimental to the national interest to emasculate a college of liberal arts unless the most pressing and urgent national necessity requires it," and expressed the opinion of the alumni that "it should not be left solely to the Navy to determine whether that existed."[12]

The public generally seemed to view what was happening as a fight between the Navy with the power of the big federal government behind it and little St. John's. Almost immediately the people of Annapolis and people all over the country took sides. The *Washington Post* and the Baltimore *Sun* in editorials opposed the Navy's taking the campus.[13] The *Post* proposed in a front page editorial that, because of the importance for national security of the naval and air bases in the Pacific, there should be established a second naval academy on the Pacific coast. Several senators from western states were in support of that proposal. Josephus Daniels, who had been Secretary of the Navy under Woodrow Wilson, in a letter to the *Post* supported a Pacific coast Academy as opposed to expanding the Academy in Annapolis. The businessmen of Annapolis became alarmed. They wanted the business that would necessarily result from doubling the brigade of midshipmen and hence greatly increasing the payroll of the Academy. They were fearful that Annapolis might lose the Naval Academy, and their fear was strengthened by a statement from Lansdale Sasscer, the Congressman for the Congressional district in which Annapolis lies, to the effect that, if a second academy were established on the west coast, "The education of midshipmen will be rapidly transferred to the West Coast Academy and Annapolis will become only a specialist or post graduate school. . . . We have got to either press for the expansion program at the Naval Academy which includes the taking of St. John's . . . or else lose the Academy." The mayor of Annapolis, William U. McCready, reminded his fellow Annapolitans that the Naval Academy brought to the community $17.5 million in annual payroll.

In the meantime Buchanan had discovered the Dartmouth College case. Dartmouth College was incorporated by royal charter in 1769. After the American Revolution and in the course of a controversy between the Republicans and the Federalists of that time the New Hampshire legislature changed the college charter in such a way as to replace the self-perpetuating body of trustees with a state-appointed body of trustees and a board of overseers. This would have transformed what had been a private college into a public one directly under the control of the state government. The state court of New Hampshire upheld the act of the legislature, but the Supreme Court of the United States reversed the decision. Chief Justice John Marshall, delivering the opinion of the Court, argued that the acts of the legislature were unconstitutional because they were in violation of Article I, Section 10 of the Constitution which declares that "no State shall . . . pass any bill . . . impairing the obligation of contracts." The royal charter was regarded as a contract establishing a corporation and therefore not subject to change by the legislature.

There is perhaps a superficial resemblance between the New Hampshire government's attempt to change the institutional character of Dartmouth

and the attempt by the Navy in 1945 to acquire the St. John's campus. In each case there was an action on the part of government against a liberal arts college. But the federal government in 1945, unlike the New Hampshire government in 1816, was not attempting to alter the terms of the charter with which the state legislature had incorporated St. John's in 1784 and hence was not "impairing the obligation of a contract." Moreover, the Naval Affairs Committees were concerned that St. John's receive adequate compensation for the campus and buildings so that the College could continue as the same incorporated entity on another site.

Buchanan, however, saw St. John's as leading a fight on behalf of all liberal arts colleges as the old trustees of Dartmouth had fought and won a fight that had implications for all liberal arts colleges in America. It was his ambition to get the United States government to abjure the exercise against liberal arts colleges of the power of eminent domain. As he wrote to his son Douglas on July 9, 1945, "The big question is whether the right of eminent domain could be challenged under the Dartmouth case. I think it could be if one wanted to build the case." Recalling that it was St. John's that in April 1945 had first suggested negotiations with the Navy, he said in a statement to the Board on July 31, 1946,

> We were important members, albeit revolutionary members, of the great liberal arts college family. We were ready to take on the responsibilities of leaders in that family, and to fight our own battle without their help if necessary or to fight their battle for them if it could be seen that way.[14]

It is a recognized principle that the federal government may exercise the power of eminent domain and acquire property whenever it is "necessary and proper" for it to do so in order to carry out any of the powers conferred on it by the Constitution,[15] and it may do that by condemnation proceedings if no other way is open. It would seem that no exception could be made in the case of liberal arts colleges. The question, however, of the necessity and propriety of the Navy's taking the St. John's campus remained.

No one voiced any desire to destroy St. John's as an invisible chartered entity or as such an entity embodied in persons and buildings. For many Annapolitans it was just a question of money. If the Academy were expanded in Annapolis that would mean more money for the town. If the federal government compensated St. John's financially in a way that would make it possible for it to continue with its liberal arts program elsewhere, why should reasonable persons object? The editor of the Annapolis *Evening Capital* did go so far as to say,

> In cold logical fact, Annapolis has been given the choice between

allowing the expansion of a great national institution, the only one of its kind in the United States and one which guards the safety of the people and a college which is but one of many similar educational institutions.[16]

On June 27, 1945, a five-man House Naval Affairs subcommittee, of which Congressman Sasscer was a member, visited Annapolis to inspect possible sites for the expansion of the Academy. They also interviewed two Annapolis real estate men to inquire about possible sites for the relocation of St. John's. The realtors suggested two sites near Annapolis. One was at Holly Beach farm, the Labrot estate at Sandy Point, nine miles away. The other was at Hillsmere on the South River, five miles away. A Baltimore architect, James R. Edmunds, who was then president of the American Institute of Architects, after studying the situation, indicated several other possibilities for the expansion of the Academy than the purchase of the St. John's campus.[17]

The St. John's board, including Barr and Buchanan, were indeed concerned, as the statement of policy of April 21, 1945, shows, with having the wherewithal to continue the function of the college on another site in the event that the Navy were to take the campus. But they meant what they said when they made removal of the college conditional upon the Navy's representing to the board that acquisition of the college property was necessary in the national interest. They may have come to mean a little more than they said, since Buchanan was soon to talk about requiring the Navy not simply to "declare" but to "find" national interest. Neither the House nor the Senate committee on naval affairs had up to this point made any formal declaration. Nor had the Secretary of the Navy. There were hearings before the committees during June 1945. Richard Cleveland, then secretary of the board, appearing before the Senate Committee on June 20, attempted to make sure that the committee understood what importance the board attached to the declaration of necessity:

> First, the Board makes clear that it will cheerfully accede to genuine national necessity if such necessity, as distinguished from convenience, is formally declared by the Navy. We now assume that the function of making such a determination and declaration of national necessity has been transferred from the Navy Department to the Congress [i.e. the Congressional committees]. The Board waives the privilege of arguing national necessity, but waives this privilege on condition that the terms of acquisition permit the Board, in its judgment, to continue to do its duty to the college community. While waiving conditionally the right for itself to argue the issue of necessity, the Board would be disap-

> pointed if the Congress did not exhaustively explore that issue. We respectfully suggest that in the distinction between necessity and convenience there is an issue much more significant in America's future than the continued life of this little college. . . .
>
> If this Committee should determine that acquisition of the College property is not in the national interest, we respectfully urge that the basis of that determination be made so explicit and so decisive that no rational persons can ever again raise the issue. We would first prefer to stay in Annapolis under conditions which would guarantee our future security. If that security is compromised, we would prefer to move to a site where no overshadowing neighbor holds the power of eminent domain. . . . If the air is once cleared, we have no fear of our ability to live near the Naval Academy in harmony and mutual respect.
>
> Perhaps this is no Dartmouth College case. But it is being watched all over this nation by citizens who hope that this war has not been fought in vain.[18]

It seems that the committees and the Navy Department still did not grasp what St. John's was after in asking for a declaration of national necessity.[19] At a meeting in Secretary Forrestal's office on July 20, 1945, at which Senator Walsh, Chairman of the Senate Committee and Congressman Vinson, Chairman of the House Committee and various naval officers were present, and after they had agreed on the project of expanding the Academy by acquiring the St. John's campus, "the Secretary suggested (and it was adopted as the course of action to be pursued) that Admiral Jacobs prepare a letter for the signature of the Secretary to the Trustees of the College outlining the results of this meeting—i.e., that because of the needs of the post-war Navy the Academy must be expanded, that the Navy intends to acquire the property by negotiation if possible, or by condemnation if necessary."[20]

I think it unlikely that the Board had received or knew of this letter when they met the following day.[21] Buchanan was obviously disappointed with what had, or had not, happened at the board meeting. For the day after, in a lengthy statement to the board, after referring to "eight years of startling success of the St. John's program," he berated the members for not pressing hard enough for a declaration about national interest. He said,

> The Statement of Policy of April 21st recognizes and embraces our highest duty as trustees in the present situation, namely to 'find' national interest. It does this by refusing to give or sell the campus or discuss damages until national interest is 'found' by due process of law . . . finding national interest allows of two courses, negotiation and condemnation. The Navy has chosen

the former. On a previous occasion [probably in 1942] we chose condemnation and the Navy withdrew.

He went on to say, "This campus is essential to this College and its defence is therefore a part of the essential obligation of its trustees." He tried to frighten the board by saying that they could possibly be indicted for not fulfilling their function as trustees, and threatened to resign from the board as a vote of lack of confidence in them.[22]

Whether there was some communication with the Navy Department or the committees during the following week is not clear. On July 27, probably as a consequence of the July 20 meeting in Forrestal's office, Senator Walsh (D. Mass.), the chairman of the Senate committee, was writing a letter to Talbot Speer, president and publisher of the *Evening Capital*. He wrote that the Senate committee had taken no action except to authorize the Navy Department to enter into negotiations with the authorities at St. John's to see if an agreement on price could be reached.[23] He affirmed his understanding that the college would remain in possession of the campus for the next academic session. A postscript shows that, no sooner had he dictated the letter, than it was brought to his attention that this would not satisfy the St. John's board. He was given the impression that what the board wanted was simply action by the two congressional committees to authorize the Navy Department to acquire the campus as distinguished from negotiation with a view to agreeing on a price. This authorization he proceeded to obtain from House Committee and a majority of the Senate committee by the next day.

On August 4 a special committee of the St. John's board meeting in Baltimore decided on the basis of published reports that the Congressional committees had not met the first of the board's conditions. They agreed that they should not at this point compromise their position by entering into any negotiations, and they requested Cleveland to seek a personal talk with Senator Walsh.

Cleveland met with Walsh on August 15 at the senator's office and, while he was trying once more to make the college's position clear, Vinson wallked in. So he got to talk with the chairmen of both committees. Apparently, almost up to this point they had believed, perhaps because of the Statement of Policy of April 21, that St. John's wanted, without any fuss, to sell the campus. They had now begun to understand that this was not the case. According to Cleveland, Senator Walsh seemed to get the point about the declaration of national necessity, although Congressman Vinson did not. Vinson "stated emphatically that he thought his committee would find national interest if that was what we wanted."[24] Both chairmen declared that the action of their committees up to that time had not authorized condemnation but only negotiation, and agreed that nothing would be done until

the Congress reconvened on September 5, after which hearings would be held. At a hearing in the fall on October 2, the Board stated flatly that they "would not willingly sell the historic campus at any price."[25]

About this time Buchanan used the *Collegian,* the student newspaper, to report to the college as follows: "With the help of Mr. Edmunds the College was resting its whole case on the architectural problem and alternative solutions [for the expansion of the Academy] instead of the campus. It should be noted that the full force of the attack [St. John's attack on the Navy] was actually Socratic irony, tending to make the Navy produce its windegg. . . .

"October 24th has been set as the day for the formal decision by the House Committee. Will the College celebrate with hemlock or a feast in the Mess Hall in Bancroft? We shall discuss immortality[26] while the ship returns from Aegina.

"Proposed toast in case it is drunk in hemlock:
>Here stood
>St. John's College
>The first liberal arts college
>To be condemned by
>The United States Government
>1784-1946
>They knew not what they did."[27]

October 24 came and went and there was no announcement from Washington. In a new formal statement of policy dated November 21, 1945, the board reviewed the events since April and asserted that it was unfortunate that the project had proceeded so far before the record could be set straight on this simple but vital point. They expressed their belief that the Navy had not proved that the acquisition of the St. John's campus was necessary in the national interest. "It is now clear," they said, "that the extensive testimony before the Committees fell far short of establishing national necessity for this unprecedented use of the power of eminent domain; that failure of the Committees to act after their long and exhaustive inquiry is in itself evidence that no such necessity exists. In the light of these developments in the long interval since the Board's statement of policy, made on April 21, 1945, that statement is no longer a realistic or relevant statement of the Board's duty as trustees, and is hereby withdrawn. The Board therefore regard the unfortunate episode as concluded, and trust that the Naval Academy and St. John's are now free to proceed in mutual respect and harmony, as neighbors, to get on with their respective functions." They urged the congressional committees to declare the acquisition not necessary in the national interest and urged the Secretary of the Navy to withdraw the project, stating their belief that the government should make a public declaration that "the Government does not intend to acquire in any manner, the campus of St. John's College."[28]

Nothing conclusive was heard from the Naval Affairs Committees or the Navy Department until well into the next year. In the meantime Paul Mellon, who had been a student at St. John's in 1940–41 and who had, by generous contributions over the years, kept the College going on a year-to-year basis, wrote to Stringfellow Barr,

> Ever since last June I have been interested in setting up an initial endowment for the St. John's Program. I have been deterred from action by doubts as to whether St. John's College could keep its campus. I have felt that if it could not, it might be more in the interest of American education to find a stronger institutional vehicle to develop the educational program which you initiated at St. John's.
>
> I am therefore placing at the disposal of the Old Dominion Foundation securities currently producing an income of $125,000 per annum, which may be used for the purpose of developing the type of education now carried on at St. John's College and for other similar purposes. I am instructing the Trustees of the Foundation that they may rely on your personal judgment as to whether St. John's can be expected to preserve the campus or whether some other college you may designate will better carry out my intention and thereby become the beneficiary of these funds.[29]

When later Mellon agreed to contribute a total endowment of $4.5 million, it looked as if St. John's College might for the first time in its history become financially secure. But the question whether it would or not depended on the outcome of the Navy affair. At the same faculty meeting at which Barr announced Mellon's intention to endow the program, whether at St. John's or elsewhere, he also announced that "the Chairman and the Secretary of the Board were requested to visit the Senate and House Committees on Naval Affairs in an attempt to clarify the relation of the College with the Navy." Evidently the committees had still not formally declared that the only possible way for the Navy to expand its facilities for training officers (it being assumed that such expansion was necessary for the security of the United States) was by acquiring the land and buildings of the college.

On June 8, 1946, Thomas Parran, the chairman of the St. John's Board, received a letter from Secretary Forrestal which read as follows:

> I have recently been informed by the Chairman of the House Naval Affairs Committee that his Committee on May 22, 1946, adopted the following resolution regarding the utilization of St. John's College Property for expansion of the Naval Academy:

'Whereas, a proposal has been made that the expanding program of the United States Naval Academy at Annapolis, Maryland, requires the acquisition of the adjoining site of St. John's College,

'Whereas the Naval Affairs Committee of the House of Representatives has held long and exhaustive hearings thereon, and

'Whereas upon careful consideration it is the sense of this committee that the National Emergency neither justifies nor warrants the proposed acquisition of St. John's campus. Now, therefore, be it resolved

'That said proposed acquisition officially known as Project No. 460C of the Real Estate Division, Bureau of Yards and Docks, Navy Department, is hereby disapproved.'

I am happy to advise you that the Navy Department acquiesces in this action of the House Naval Affairs Committee. The Department was most reluctant to undertake the acquisition of the college property for the required expansion of the Naval Academy in Annapolis since the Department recognizes that only considerations of extreme national necessity would justify the taking of the campus of a liberal arts college. . . .

It is believed that the present considerations of the House Naval Affairs Committee and the Department . . . coupled with the fact that the Department has other plans for the expansion of the Academy in Annapolis, make it possible for the college to pursue its plans with assurance that it will be secure on its historic site for the foreseeable future. . . .

A few days after Forrestal's letter the Senate Naval Affairs Committee followed the example of the House Committee. Dr. Parran observed that this action consequent upon the House Committee's resolution and the secretary's letter, drove "the third nail in the coffin" of the project to take the campus.

Cleveland, who knew that Barr and Buchanan wanted from the Congressional committees a strong statement that it was not the policy of the United States government to use the power of eminent domain against liberal arts colleges, had been engaged in some activity behind the scenes to get from the House committee a statement that would satisfy them and keep them with the program at St. John's in Annapolis. He even persuaded Carl Vinson, chairman of the House Committee, who had already written a letter saying that the committee's resolution wrote "Finis" to the project, to write a second stronger letter. But in spite of the death and burial of the project, and in spite of this stronger letter, and in spite of Forrestal's declara-

tion that only extreme national necessity would warrant the government's taking the property of a liberal arts college, and in spite of the assurance given about the foreseeable future, Barr, after consulting with Buchanan, decided that the securities promised by Mellon should not come to St. John's. He suggested to the board that the St. John's campus be turned over to the State of Maryland to provide educational facilities for the state since the state would be better able to protect the campus and that the board should seek a safe place for the college. In the event that the board did not accept his suggestion he would resign and "seek another college for the program." Buchanan had said the year before that the campus was essential to the college, and Barr had said that it was doubtful whether the college could "survive transplanting." Now they were saying something else.

Barr has always maintained that he was not satisfied that the Navy had given any substantial assurance that there would not be another attempt to take the campus.[30] But that was not his only reason, and probably not his principal reason, for taking the money elsewhere. He thought that he could not dispense with the help of Buchanan in continuing the program on another site under the charter of St. John's or in establishing the program at another college.[31] Buchanan would probably have left St. John's even if the fray with the Navy had not occurred. In early January 1945 he was already beginning to withdraw from the full exercise of the office of Dean. At the first faculty meeting of that year he reported that new adult education duties he had taken on in the District of Columbia would necessitate the reduction of his decanal duties. On January 18, 1945, Barr sent a memorandum to the treasurer instructing him that the dean's salary had, at the dean's request, been reduced by the board from $5,000 a year to $3,000 a year in view of other salaried employment undertaken in Washington. He would continue as "the officer of instruction", i.e., as chairman of the Instruction Committee, and as adviser to students in relation to their studies. Buchanan himself in a letter to Cleveland about two years later wrote: "If things had gone as usual, I would have resigned during this year [1945–46] to go into adult education or something else. I never was made for an administrator." On June 1, 1946, he announced that he would take a year's leave of absence. It seemed clear to everyone that the unique role he had played for the eight years that he had portrayed as "eight years of startling success" was coming to an end. In addition to that, as Barr describes it, while he himself was exhausted from the fight with the Navy, Buchanan was both tired and sick.[32]

The board had, since 1937, been guided in practically everything by Barr and Buchanan. They failed, however, to concur in the opinion that there was just as much danger as ever that the Navy would soon again seek possession of the St. John's campus. They were unwilling to abandon the campus and move the college and the program, and they were also unwill-

ing to resign as trustees of St. John's and become trustees of some other college yet to be chartered in Maryland or some other state. They had been convinced by Barr and Buchanan of the worth of the program, and they were resolved to continue it at St. John's and in Annapolis. They tried, but failed, to persuade Barr and Buchanan to reconsider.

Buchanan professed surprise at the board's decision. In fact, in a memorandum of July 31, 1946, addressed to them he declared that it was "surprising to all" that the board had decided to continue the St. John's program in Annapolis "even when it was clear that the original pilots could not honestly take the risk as they saw it and weighed it."[33] He, nevertheless, spoke of the ready respect commanded by the board's insight and courage, but also asserted that the board's action did not "convince the ex-pilots that their return would be safe or wise." He already had plans for a larger enterprise which would grow from the cooperation of St. John's and the new college. The aim was the eventual establishment of a university which would be composed of (1) a graduate school for research in the "liberal arts and philosophy," (2) an adult school with many communities, and (3) several undergraduate colleges. For the immediate future the new college somewhere other than at Annapolis would, with the Mellon gift as endowment, be a "small model of the whole." In addition to a small undergraduate school, it would include a committee on the liberal arts to become a nucleus of the graduate school, "and it would be situated in a place suitable for "cooperation with a lively industrial community in adult education." He even suggested that for a certain period of transition there be one board and one president for St. John's and the new institution.

Looking back over the nine years, he commented on the successes and failures of the program. While denying once more that the program was an experiment designed to prove or disprove an hypothesis, he affirmed that there had been a common search for a true liberal arts college and that the search was based on guiding principles and a common comprehensive sphere for exploration. There had been found a pattern of the liberal arts as embodied in the great books and it had proved to be "workable, versatile, instructive, fruitful, and heuristic." He spoke of the "high level of teaching and learning we had already achieved before the war" as well as of serious sickness caused by the war. The case for the endowment could now be based, he maintained, on achievement rather than "mere paper promises."

The Navy affair itself he cited as evidence of the college's growth and strength. He assigned as a reason for the college's suggesting negotiations with the Navy in the statement of April 21, 1945, the desire to "discover and clarify the foundations of our own existence." He meant more than the particular and local factors affecting the existence of St. John's. He meant, as he had said earlier, that St. John's had been leading a fight on behalf of all liberal arts colleges insofar as their existence depends upon the policies of the federal government.

A few days after this memorandum of Buchanan's the board made public the following announcement:

> The Board wishes to record publicly its deep satisfaction at the favorable termination of the Navy Department's proposal to acquire the campus of St. John's College and joins heartily in the gratification expressed by Secretary Forrestal that this solution will make it possible for the College and the Naval Academy to continue their long history as friendly neighbors. . . .
>
> The Board believes that this solution . . . places the College in a stronger position than it has been in its long history to press forward with plans for the future. . . .
>
> The firm foundation now achieved in Annapolis also makes it possible sometime in the near future, to further the establishment elsewhere of an additional college to carry on the program developed and now secure in Annapolis. Fortunately a generous gift for this purpose makes it practicable. . . .
>
> In furtherance of this project the Board has agreed to release Mr. Barr from the presidency of St. John's College as of July 1, 1947, or such other date as may be determined, in order that he may take over the leadership of the proposed new college.[34]

Buchanan in a letter to Adler gave his own very different account of what had happened:

> The Board, primarily Dick Cleveland, had not earlier imagined, say nothing of believed, that Winkie was actually thinking of weighing old St. John's and making an objective decision on his findings. They therefore had thought only of their and his efforts to set things straight in Annapolis and were themselves ready to settle for anything that the Navy and the Congressional Committees would do; no one in his right mind will refuse four and a half million dollars because of an uncertain future.[35]

He proceeded to describe a meeting in Paul Mellon's office in Washington at which he and Barr were present together with Mellon, Adolph Schmidt, and Thomas Parran. Parran spoke for the Board. Buchanan's version of what he said is as follows:

> First the Board was determined to continue the St. John's Program in Annapolis; I am sure this implied that the program, like the library for instance, was the property of the Board, copyrighted and patented in the name of the College. We would be stealing if we took it elsewhere and taught it, and they would

tell the public so. Second, Winkie was tired and probably sick like me, and he ought to take a leave of absence this year to recover his right mind and allow the decision to be postponed. Third, if Winkie insisted on accepting the endowment to go elsewhere, he should give it to some institution with which he would have no personal connection. Parran delivered these threats in the presence of Mellon and Schmidt. They behaved admirably. . . . Mellon and Schmidt were very clear about their original intention and their full confidence in Winkie.

At the November faculty meeting in 1946 Barr announced the formation of a foundation to be known as Liberal Arts Incorporated to be a formal instrument for acquiring property for the new college.[36] He further stated that Liberal Arts Incorporated might eventually become a "higher governing board for both colleges." At the December meeting he informed the faculty that the site of the new college would be the Hanna estate in the Stockbridge Bowl in western Massachusetts, that his resignation would take effect on December 31, 1946, and that John S. Kieffer had been appointed acting president by the board.

By this time Buchanan had left and was living in Richmond, Massachusetts, not far from Stockbridge. In a letter to Richard Cleveland in late November he made as a tentative proposal that Liberal Arts Incorporated take over the financial and educational direction of St. John's from the trustees "exactly as Winkie and I had taken it in 1937 except that this time we would recommend other personnel to do the job on the spot."[37] He added, "I wish with all my heart that the Board had had confidence in Winkie and me and had wished to come with us. . . . The new enterprise has lost immeasurably by the Board's refusal to come with us. We have some money but we have lost a college. I saw that this was so and that it was intended to be so when you read your announcement to us. Winkie and I have lost nine years of work unless you and the Board relent and give us some help. I am not regretting our decision but I am suggesting that you are making the cost maximum." The board of St. John's made no response to the proposal that Liberal Arts Incorporated be given responsibilities that were not properly theirs.

Shortly thereafter, in a letter to Hutchins, Buchanan recorded his reflections about what had happened at St. John's.[38] He claimed that a controlled search for a liberal college had been started, that some liberal arts had been set into motion within a framework of great books, that there was enough initial success to justify that kind of practice and that certain things had to be added, such as the graduate school to sharpen the focus on subject matter, and full commitment to adult education. "It is also clear," he went on, "that the next thirty or forty years offer a desperately receptive world for

us to bring light to. As I have said in print, this is the day of the liberal college which has been waiting for twenty-four hundred years to be born." In the same letter he says "we don't know what we have been studying and teaching, and we ought to find out."

The inconsistencies in Buchanan's statements make it difficult to know what he was thinking. On the one hand, he had reported to the board that the first eight years of the program were "eight years of startling success." On the other hand, he says that he and Barr will have "lost nine years of work" if the board don't follow in his footsteps. On the one hand he says he doesn't know what he's been studying and teaching. But on the other, he thinks that he and his associates will bring light not just to a few who might be interested in "the liberal college," but to the world. Presumably he means more than a little light, since it is something that the world has been waiting for since the time of Plato and Aristotle.

Buchanan tried to get his old friends, Adler and McKeon, to join him and Barr in Massachusetts. He also tried to get Hutchins, Van Doren, and Meiklejohn to leave what they were doing and join the new enterprise. All refused. A few of the St. John's faculty were invited; they too refused, believing that the outcome of the contest with the Navy was decisive and that there was much more uncertainty about the new college than about the future of St. John's in Annapolis. Liberal Arts Incorporated, as Acting President Kieffer announced to the faculty on January 11, 1947, would contribute $150,000 to meet the operating deficit that year at St. John's. It was understood that this would fulfill the intention of Liberal Arts Incorporated to cause as few difficulties as possible for St. John's, and that by the summer of 1948 the two colleges would be independent but free to enter into any form of cooperation that might at that time seem wise.

It became clear early in 1947, less than a month after Barr's departure from St. John's, that he was running into difficulties in founding the new college. On January 25, he wrote to Paul Mellon, "The size of the endowment was measured to fit an entirely different problem from the new one we now face. It would have run St. John's well. But St. John's already had a campus, a plant in good order, and equipment." Around the middle of the year he requested Mellon to release the entire benefits of the endowment fund to Liberal Arts Incorporated for other use than the establishment of an undergraduate college. Mellon refused to do so on the ground that it had been his intention only to endow a "college for undergraduates similar in size and curriculum to St. John's." He noted in a letter to Barr of June 24, 1947, "Through circumstances beyond your control that project now appears unfeasible, if not impossible, within any reasonable amount of time, chiefly due to lack of qualified teachers and adequate building funds."[39] Barr, however, has claimed that the whole effort was sabotaged by Donald Shepard, who, as vice-president of Mellon's Old Dominion Foundation, had

a good deal to do with the terms of the disposal of the funds.[40] It was announced to the St. John's faculty at the first fall meeting in 1947 that on August 1 Liberal Arts Incorporated had met in Stockbridge and decided to abandon the project of a new college. "Unpropitiousness of building," it was said, "and difficulties of cooperating with the Old Dominion Foundation were the chief reasons for the decision."[41] The endowment fund reverted to the Old Dominion Foundation.

Thus ended the last attempt of Barr and Buchanan to form an institution which would be a beacon for colleges and universities to follow. They did not in the succeeding years keep in close touch with St. John's College and knew very little about what was happening at St. John's. There were a few times when they returned, upon invitation, to lecture or to speak at Class Day or Commencement. One such occasion was Class Day in 1948 when both Barr and Buchanan spoke. Buchanan in his speech urged that the liberal arts should have a subject matter and that the core of the St. John's curriculum should be, not metaphysical (which had earlier been his constant theme), but political. A few days later, when he had returned to Massachusetts, he wrote President Kieffer a letter in which he told him that the decision that Kieffer and the board made to continue the program in Annapolis was "stupid and blind and therefore highly irresponsible to the vision, highly misleading to the community, and disloyal to whatever leadership Winkie and I provided."[42] He claimed that the original program was "a revolutionary blueprint to subvert and rebuild education, that it was a bull-dozer inside a Trojan horse which was to be let loose once the walls of the sacred city were passed and left behind." He said, "I fought the Navy fight, with the few who cared out of piety to the sacred city" but that "there were no reinforcements, only those who were non-combatants and had a sentimental wish to live in the ruins." He maintained, presumably referring to the agreement that St. John's should have the income from the Mellon endowment until July 1, 1948, that he and Barr had "a fit of personal generosity which did not blind them but blurred their vision, and that out of their clear vision of what was the only hope for the program together with their blurred vision produced by the board's bad decision had come the ordeal of Stockbridge which could only commit suicide because of its high courage and generosity to St. John's." He said that "the program should be laid on the shelf and forgotten, that it was not even a pattern to be laid up in heaven and beheld, but a poison corrupting a household at St. John's and that because of its being at St. John's it would become a poison wherever it was tried." He asserted that he and Barr had made "a mistaken historical judgment in 1937 and a bad educational prediction and that they should be counted out of any plans that Kieffer and the people at St. John's might make."

Scott Buchanan had over a period of twenty years invested an enormous

amount of love and work in formulating, planning, and trying to bring into being, whether at St. John's or elsewhere, what had come to be called the St. John's program. At this point it seemed to him that it had all come to nothing. The tragedy, if it is to be dignified by that name, is not that he had failed, or that the program had failed, or that others had failed him, but rather that he would not question the wisdom of actions that, by denying the college the endowment it otherwise would have had, jeopardized the existence of the only college where had been established, however precariously, the program for which he more than anyone was responsible, and furthermore that he never knew to what extent he had laid the foundations for a building that through many vicissitudes, was to increase in worth.

Barr, reflecting upon these events many years later, could say of his decision to leave St. John's and to use the Mellon money to start another college, "I don't claim for a second I made a wise choice."[43]

CHAPTER 7

Kieffer's Presidency and the Beginning of Weigle's

Stringfellow Barr's successor as president of St. John's was John S. Kieffer, who had joined the faculty as instructor in classical languages in 1929. Barr had, while still in office, strongly recommended Richard Cleveland as his successor on the ground of his familiarity with the program and his ability to interpret it and the college to the people of Maryland. When Cleveland declined, Barr advocated the appointment of Kieffer as acting president. With the concurrence of the Instruction Committee of the faculty the board appointed Kieffer acting president, and he took office on January 1, 1947. There seems to have been some reluctance on the part of the board to place Kieffer in the position of president. Scott Buchanan wrote to Richard Cleveland later in January: "I rather hope that he [Kieffer] can be made president at the end of the year. In that case I for one would be willing to return to membership on the Board."[1] Cleveland replied, "I am a Kieffer fan. There is no denying that his difficulty in speech is a handicap for the chief administrative officer of a college—leaving out money raising!"[2] Kieffer, who was as thoroughly dedicated to the St. John's program as anyone, was rather slow of speech, and for that reason sometimes had difficulty holding the attention of a listener. He had had no experience in money raising. The board, however, on April 22, 1947, elected him president of the college.

It soon became apparent that he saw himself as replacing both Barr and Buchanan. The occasion to do this arose because John O. Neustadt, who upon his return from military service in World War II had ably served as acting dean for the 1946–47 session, had just resigned; at about the same time Kieffer was elected president. Kieffer then recommended for appointment as dean Raymond N. Wilburn who had been a member of the faculty since 1938 and had served as assistant dean under Buchanan. In announcing this appointment, he set forth for the board and the faculty a redefinition of the duties and offices of the administrative members of the college

faculty. The president was to direct the program of instruction and to be chairman of the Instruction Committee while the dean was to be concerned with the details of the program, with such things as reading schedules, academic standing, and admissions.

This was a quite different arrangement from that embodied in the polity which Barr had made the governing constitution of the college by presidential fiat in 1945. Although at that time it had not been approved by the faculty, it was so approved on June 12, 1946, while Barr was still president and recommended by the faculty to the board for approval, rejection, or amendment. The board, however, had not acted by the time Barr had left and Kieffer, now president, had announced his redefinition of duties and offices. Upon receiving this announcement, the faculty voted to withdraw its approval of the polity and the recommendation of the polity to the board. This left the college without a polity during the two years of Kieffer's presidency, although he did assign the Instruction Committee the task of writing a new polity and at a faculty meeting of January 8, 1948, suggested that the new polity should be "a written formulation of the existing non-written polity."[3] That is, he wanted the new polity to reflect the arrangement of offices and duties that he had already decreed.

Shortly after that Kieffer gave the board a report on the state of the college that was on the whole encouraging. He informed the board that the faculty was reacting favorably to what the college was trying to do, but that many students seemed to be bewildered and overwhelmed by the amount of work they had to do and that some were inclined to look back on the mythical age of Barr and Buchanan and compare it with the present. He declared it his opinion that the college was doing a better job than ever before, particularly in the work of the seminars.

Certain curricular changes were made during Kieffer's presidency. In line with a general tendency throughout the history of the program to read less and to read better, the seminar reading list was revised to include fewer books. Latin had been abandoned as the language to be studied in the second year so that now, instead of the four-year sequence of Greek, Latin, French, and German, there were two years of Greek, one year of German, and one year of French, in that order. The reason for this change was that, although there was never the claim that in one year the student would master the language and although it was intended that the center of attention should be the function of language as such rather than learning a particular language, it had become the prevailing opinion that this purpose would be better served by allotting more time to just one of the ancient languages. With some regret because of the role of Latin in the genesis of the English language, the decision was made in favor of two years of Greek. The reasons for this were the greater "flexibility and expressiveness" of Greek and the more important part that books originally written in Greek have played in human thought. The Greek of the first year remained unchanged. The Greek

Fabian Bachrach

John S. Kieffer.

of the second year was devoted to fostering a more precise understanding of certain texts that were read also for seminar discussion. There was to be a review of Greek grammar followed by translation from the New Testament and from parts of Aristotle's *Metaphysics,* Book XII.

In the laboratory, the separation of the sciences that had begun under Buchanan, and which he had reluctantly allowed, continued. It was easy to share Buchanan's desire to unify the sciences and to integrate them with the rest of the curriculum. To accomplish those two things was not easy. Nor was it easy to follow Buchanan's lead in these matters. The faculty who were responsible for teaching the laboratory sciences fell back more and more upon conventional textbooks. One that the students tended to ridicule was a text in chemistry by Engelder, Dunkelberger, and Schiller. Actually it was not a bad text for learning chemistry, but it did not do much in the way of relating chemistry to the question of being *qua* being.

Kieffer and Wilburn instituted a forum for the discussion of the curriculum with the students, but this does not seem to have helped much as far as the laboratory was concerned. The students' *Nineteen Forty-eight Yearbook* reported, "The laboratory was a problem about which most of us were mystified and about which none of us talked very well. Despite the efforts of Mr. Kieffer and Mr. Wilburn to clarify the relations between the laboratory and the rest of the liberal arts curriculum at the newly instituted forum discussions, the dialectic was murky and tended to degenerate when the time came for questions. Here as in other cases communication failed because of the extremes of too-lofty abstraction and too-irrelevant complaints about particular features of the laboratory against which one or a few students might harbor an animus."[4]

Music as part of the curriculum began to come into its own with the appointment of Victor Zuckerkandl to the faculty in 1948. Zuckerkandl, a native of Austria and a refugee from Hitler, not only understood music well but had good ideas about how to lead students in searching out what is meaningful or intelligible in music. He persuaded the Instruction Committee to increase the number of music seminars. It became the practice for the faculty and students who took part in those seminars to prepare for them by listening to and following with a score whatever music was to be discussed, whether the St. Matthew Passion, Mozart's *Don Giovanni,* Beethoven's Ninth Symphony, or something else. Zuckerkandl also got the instruction committee to introduce a special music tutorial in which the students might learn fundamental things about pitch, meter, and rhythm and to recognize the musical intervals, and dynamic tendencies of tones, and their relations in the scale.

It was during Kieffer's presidency that black students were admitted to St. John's for the first time. Barr had in 1944 rejected an application from a black student named William Washington on the ground that he "would

not find life in Annapolis pleasant or conducive to good scholarship because of racial segregation practiced in Annapolis."[5] In early April 1948 a student poll indicated that the students were overwhelmingly in favor of the admission of black students. On April 10, Winfree Smith moved in faculty meeting that "the faculty go on record as favoring the admission of negro students as a matter of College policy." The motion passed unanimously. The board, however, meeting a week later, stated their general agreement with the substance of the letter Barr had written to William Washington. Shortly thereafter a black student, Martin Dyer, applied for admission. Kieffer at the July meeting of the board gave it as his opinion that Dyer's application should be accepted and said that he felt "that to refuse to admit a Negro to St. John's would be inconsistent with the liberal education which is being taught at the college and would be bad for the morale of students and faculty." The board, however, voted 9 to 3 to reject Dyer's appication. On September 17, 1948, the Executive Committee of the board reversed that decision, just in time for Dyer to enroll as a student.

Kieffer's term as president of the college came to a rather abrupt end. Sometime in late November 1948 the dean, Raymond Wilburn, the assistant dean, Harvey Poe, and the treasurer, Harrison Fiddesof, went to Richard Cleveland, the chairman of the board, with the charge that Kieffer was a failure as a president and that the stability of the college would be seriously threatened by his continuance in office. The principal failing, from their point of view, had to do with administrative matters. Indecision and the inability to hold to decisions once made were among the charges. Cleveland, in discussing Kieffer's presidency with Wilburn and Poe, admitted that he and others on the board had grave doubts about Kieffer's suitability as president and suggested that no action should be taken until the board could decide on what steps to take in replacing Kieffer. Although Cleveland and the board had the matter under consideration for over two months, they did not take any action or inform Kieffer of the conversation with Cleveland, which gave the whole affair the aspect of a conspiracy. Kieffer was finally informed of it by Wilburn in late January, whereupon he asked and received the resignations of Wilburn and Poe. Since Fiddesof had not been appointed by him, but by the board, only the board could require his resignation. The board then investigated the situation and, after hearing from both faculty and students, decided to terminate Kieffer's presidency. On January 30, 1949, they issued the following statement:

> The Board has been considering for the past two days a serious problem raised by differences of opinion on purely administrative problems among Mr. Kieffer on the one hand and the other three administrative officers on the other, namely Mr. Wilburn as Dean, Mr. Poe as Assistant Dean, and Mr. Fiddesof

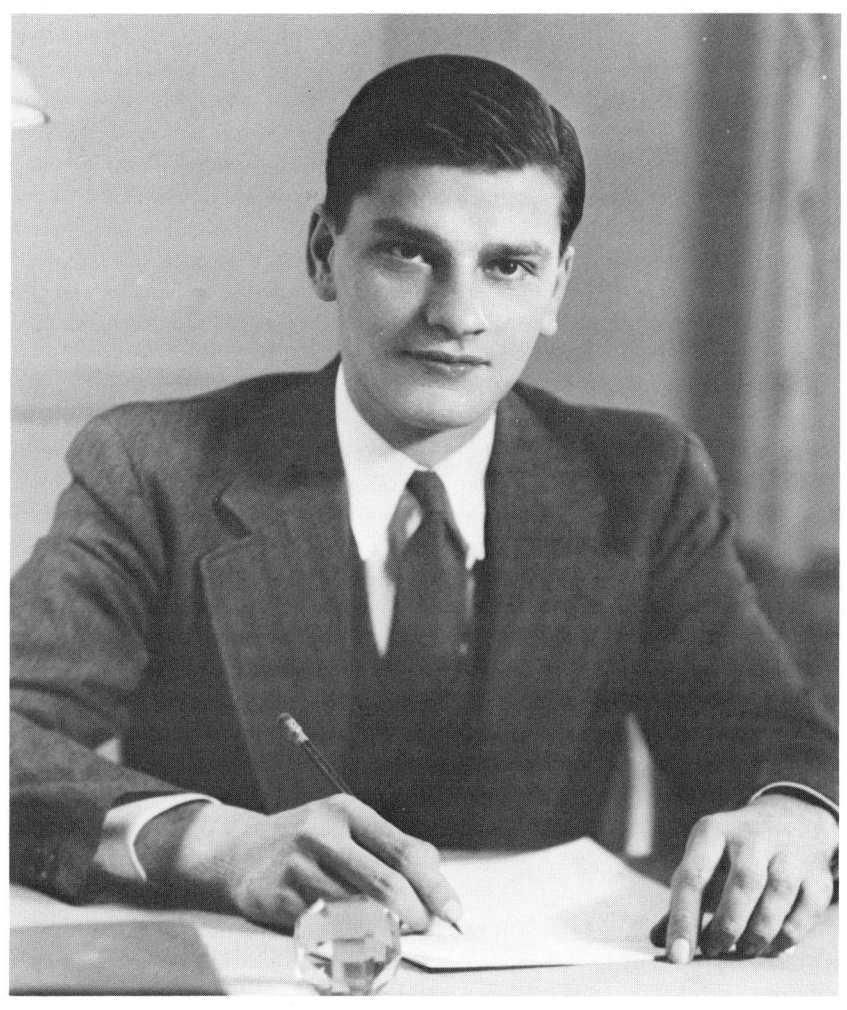

Raymond N. Wilburn.

as Treasurer. We have taken counsel with the faculty and have received communications oral and written from students. Mr. Wilburn and Mr. Poe as appointees of the president have resigned on January 24th at the president's request. Mr. Fiddesof held his office by election of the Board. . . . On the departure of Mr. Barr and Mr. Buchanan the faculty recommended that Mr. Kieffer be made acting president and he took that position in January 1947 and was subsequently made president. He was virtually drafted for a type of function which he did not seek, but his long and able and valuable service as a member of the faculty made him its logical choice at that critical point. The Board acknowledges in retrospect that it was a disservice to Mr. Kieffer to inject him into a position in which his splendid personal and professional qualities did not function most fruitfully.

No question about the instructional program itself or the personal qualities of the four administrative officers have been involved in the consideration of the problem by the Board.[6]

Thus the board somewhat obliquely acknowledged that it had made a mistake in choosing Kieffer as president. Kieffer, Wilburn, and Poe were to continue as members of the faculty. Fiddesof resigned as treasurer which in effect meant his leaving the college. It is no doubt true that, in addition to the kind of administrative difficulties mentioned, Wilburn also found it difficult to function as Kieffer's subordinate in the direction and execution of the curriculum. In some ways he was the logical successor to Buchanan. He had been a student of Buchanan's in philosophy at the University of Virginia and one of his most enthusiastic admirers. After a year of graduate work at Columbia, he had been brought by Buchanan to St. John's to be assistant dean. In that capacity he had been very close to Buchanan in the early years when the program was getting established. It is, therefore, possible that he was dissatisfied with Kieffer's handling of the curriculum, although such dissatisfaction did not appear in any public statement.

At the same time that the chairman of the board announced the resignations of the four administrative officers of the college, he announced that Kieffer would continue as president until the end of the current academic session, that Wilburn would go on sabbatical leave, and that Poe might have a leave of absence. Jacob Klein, he reported, had been appointed acting dean and chairman of the Instruction Committee. Klein had been a member of the faculty since 1938. Although the appointment of a new president was the prerogative of the board, Klein and a committee of the faculty but especially Klein, had a large hand in his selection. At a meeting of the board on March 19, 1949, Klein urged upon the board that the new president should be well acquainted with the meaning and scope of the St. John's pro-

gram and voiced the fear that, without such familiarity, the person selected might allow the college to slide to the conventional level. He suggested that the board's search committee be enlarged to include some faculty members. The faculty had as their primary concern that the future president should be sufficiently well acquainted with the meaning of the program to be an intelligent and knowledgeable spokesman for it. One way to help secure this was to have the faculty through their representation participate in the choice. The faculty, therefore, elected a committee consisting of Klein, Kieffer, Ford K. Brown, and J. Winfree Smith to assist the board's committee. At the time of their election Klein named as possible candidates for the presidency Richard Cleveland, Mark Van Doren, and Lewis Hammond. Hammond had been associated with Buchanan in the philosophy faculty at the University of Virginia and had been a tutor at St. John's for two years, returning later to Virginia. For various reasons all three declined.

On September 17, 1949, Richard D. Weigle was elected president of St. John's by unanimous vote of the board and was to perform the duties of that office for thirty-one years. The son of Luther Weigle, dean of the Yale Divinity School and chairman of the committee that produced the Revised Standard Version of the Bible, Richard Weigle attended Yale University, taught English at Yale in China, returned to Yale to get a doctorate in 1939 in American diplomatic history, taught for a while at Carleton College in Minnesota, and wound up as executive officer in the Office of Far Eastern Affairs at the State Department before coming to St. John's. By way of helping the board decide whether they wanted him as president, he wrote to Richard Cleveland, the chairman, as follows:

> There are certain points upon which the Board would undoubtedly wish to have some expression of opinion from me. In the first place, I am heartily in accord with the program at St. John's College and believe that it can make and is making a great contribution to the educational world. I would feel committed to the principles upon which the program is based but would hope that the curriculum might retain a degree of flexibility so that it could be modified as experience and other factors might dictate. . . .
>
> I should expect that a considerable portion of the time of the President would be devoted to public relations and personnel work. There would appear to be no insuperable obstacles in winning for the College its proper place, whether with respect to the community or the Naval Academy in the city of Annapolis, or with respect to the State of Maryland or the broader educational circle of the nation. I would think that accreditation would come in time as the College attained a firmer financial and administrative base.

> The finances of the College do not appear unduly difficult. I recognize that there must be some major giving to meet building and endowment needs. I should expect the cooperation of the Board in the matter of making appropriate contacts, if large potential sources of giving are to be tapped. The actual business of money-raising, I recognize as the responsibility of the President.
>
> It is easy to understand the heat that has been generated in the Board by the question of negro admissions. I should make it clear that I would not consider race or creed to be a bar to any student seeking admission, should his scholastic record and personal characteristics warrant such admission. It would appear to me that there is basically no very great problem, for the number of qualified negro students interested in the St. John's program is never likely to be large. . . .
>
> I believe that I would undertake the job with a deep-seated religious motivation, even though that might at times lack open expression. I do not think that this would necessarily take a Calvinistic or puritanical turn, and I should always strive for broad-minded understanding and a judicious degree of flexibility. . . .[7]

This letter, first of all, was intended to reassure any who might have doubts about Weigle's allegiance to the program. During all his years as president of St. John's, he defended the program publicy. He left the actual determination of curricular matters to the dean and Instruction Committee, making suggestions now and then but never interfering or using his presidential authority to overrule. Some of the alumni who had been students in the early years of the program missed in him the éclat that characterized Stringfellow Barr. He made up for that by good sense and fair-mindedness as well as by diligence in the performance of his duties.

From this letter we also sense that he intended to foster amicable relationships with the city of Annapolis, with the Naval Academy, and with other colleges. He was not going to offend any of the citizens of Annapolis by making them the butt of his wit, as Barr sometimes did. While defending the St. John's curriculum he was not going to attack other colleges as inferior or worthless or worse than worthless. This desire for peace with the rest of the world, including the educational world, as well as his concern that the college's accreditation be restored, made some of the alumni uneasy lest he might gradually turn the college into an ordinary "respectable" institution.

The paragraph in Weigle's letter about the admission of black students was prompted by the fact that in the summer before Weigle took office and even after Martin Dyer's application had been accepted, there were heated discussions within the board which showed that for many members the issue

of admitting blacks was not yet settled. At their May meeting in 1949, the board voted not to accept an award granted to the college by the Sidney Hollander Foundation for the college's contribution toward bringing about a better relationship between the white and Negro races by the admission of Martin Dyer. Weigle's letter made his position clear on the matter of principle, and no doubt had much to do with the fact that since 1949 the admission of black students has been accepted as a matter of course. Time has shown that Weigle was right in his prediction that very few blacks would apply to become students at St. John's, though one may regret that it should have been given as a reason for admitting blacks that there would not be many of them anyway. It may be that young black people, if they think about St. John's at all, see it as a school that will be of little use in helping them make successful careers in a society which for so long placed obstacles in the way of their advancement.

Weigle's words concerning his religious motivation should be taken seriously. Twice during his presidency motions were introduced in faculty meetings to do away with the annual baccalaureate service on the ground that a college that has no religious commitment is pretending to be what it is not when, if only once a year, it engages in communal worship. Weigle both times vigorously and successfully opposed the motions, stating that he would resign if the baccalaureate service were abolished and on one occasion that in his opinion the college as such was committed to belief in a God who listens to and answers petitionary prayer. There is no doubt that he thought of his presidency as, in some sense, a religious calling. Why he wished to reassure the board that his religious motivation would not take a Calvinistic or puritanical turn is not clear; perhaps he thought that his Protestant New England background might have aroused some speculation within the board.

The new president immediately went to work at the task of raising funds necessary for the maintenance of the college. At the very next meeting after the one at which he was elected he proposed a financial campaign to raise $10 million, of which $7.5 million would be endowment and $2.5 million would go for buildings. The buildings needed were a new heating plant, a new dormitory, a science building, and an auditorium. At a meeting in January 1950, the board approved the financial campaign, setting a goal of $7 million instead of $10 million. It was not clear at this time whether Paul Mellon or the Old Dominion Foundation would continue to support the college financially. After the failure of Barr and Buchanan to establish another college in Massachusetts, Mellon did keep the college solvent through Kieffer's administration. Mark Van Doren's report of a conversation he had with Mellon in January 1948 shows that Mellon was still concerned about the financial needs of the college and was not too much worried about the Navy's making another attempt to acquire the St. John's campus. He and

the other trustees of the Old Dominion Foundation, however, did want to encourage support on a large scale from other sources. Therefore, the Old Dominion Foundation, though it made certain outright grants for specific purposes, began in 1950 and continued for a decade to pledge sums for buildings and endowment on the condition that these sums be matched with equal amounts from other donors.

Weigle met the challenge. By 1952 a new heating plant had been erected; by 1954 a new dormitory. At the time the new dormitory, Campbell Hall, was built, plans were already begun for what was to be the greatest building project of Weigle's presidency, a building which would contain a large auditorium together with laboratories and other facilities for the study of the sciences. The board decided that the development of the upper or front campus, facing the street, should be along traditional lines, but that the development of the back campus toward College Creek should be in horizontal contemporary style. A contract was signed with Neutra and Alexander as architects to design the auditorium and science building for the back campus. The result was a splendid example of modern architecture, which was so designed as to harmonize perfectly with the eighteenth-century style of McDowell Hall and other buildings in Annapolis. This building was completed in 1958, the auditorium being named for Francis Scott Key, who was an alumnus of St. John's, and the science building for Paul Mellon. President Dwight D. Eisenhower spoke at its dedication. While seeking money for these needed buildings, Weigle was at the same time seeking to increase the college's endowment. When he became president there was virtually no endowment. By 1955 the endowment fund had a market value of $844,715; by 1958 the market value was $2,435,503. This was made possible, of course, partly through the unfailing generosity of Paul Mellon and partly through the generosity of those whom Weigle got to contribute matching funds.

Then there was the question of accreditation. The examining committee of the accrediting association, the Middle States Association of Colleges and Secondary Schools, had indicated that one of the principal obstacles to restoration of St. John's accreditation, which had been withdrawn under President Woodcock, was the financial instability of the college. Weigle was hoping already in the early part of 1953 that, as the college became more stable financially, the accrediting association would act favorably on the college's accreditation. On May 18 he was able to inform the board that the college's application for accreditation had been approved.

The reason that he considered it important for St. John's to recover its accreditation was that he believed that the lack of accreditation was a major factor in the difficulty the college was having obtaining students. The enrollment had increased from 165 in the session of 1945–46 to 253 in the next session because of the veterans returning to college after World War II. But

two or three years later it began to drop and steadily declined until the session of 1953–54 when only 40 freshmen were admitted and the total enrollment was 125. Whether Weigle was right in seeing a connection between lack of accreditation and low enrollment is a question. Just before the college recovered its accreditation the director of admissions had sent out a questionnaire to 192 prospective students who had decided not to come to St. John's. Of the 103 who replied,

- 44 wanted to specialize
- 25 found the expenses too great
- 17 had no interest in the program
- 14 objected because the college was not accredited
- 11 said it was too far from their home
- 9 wanted intercollegiate athletics
- 4 wanted credit for previous college courses
- 3 found their parents opposed.

It is worthy of note that more than half of these replies have to do with the program. We do not know how well informed about the program these 61 were. It may be that the St. John's program would have had then, and would have now, an attraction for a greater number of American youth if they had been, or were, better informed. Whether it would ever be widely popular remains a question.

Although the faculty and board were convinced of the simple justice of admitting women to St. John's on the same basis as men, there seems to be little doubt that the declining enrollment had much to do with Weigle's initiative in leading the board in December 1950 to decide to admit women students the following year. The first appointment of a woman to the faculty had been made by Barr in February 1940. Helen Hill Miller, wife of Francis Miller and a distinguished economist then with the Agriculture Department and Secretary of the National Policy Committee, was appointed to teach a class in economics to old program students. The hope was expressed that she would remain to teach in the new program. She, however, decided otherwise, and the college remained without any women on the faculty until, with the admission of women students in 1951, Barbara Leonard was appointed tutor and assistant dean. Since then many women have joined the faculty under a policy which allows no discrimination on the basis of sex.

CHAPTER 8

Jacob Klein, Dean

At the time that Jacob Klein became acting dean the college was shaken by the painful events that had led to the resignations of Kieffer and Wilburn. Although Kieffer remained in office until the end of the academic session, the acting dean was in effect the person in command. On the day that the chairman of the board announced Kieffer's resignation, Klein addressed the faculty and students as follows:

> This is certainly not the right occasion for a grand speech. And even if it was, I could hardly deliver it out of sheer physical exhaustion. What all of us need, or most of us, at any rate, is a good night of sound sleep. I, for one, feel very strongly about that.
>
> Let me, therefore, be very brief. The events of the last weeks will not leave us, the college community, unscathed. I suppose nobody has any illusions on that score. Let us all try to pour *some* oil on *too* stormy waters. I'll do my best, and I'm sure of your help which I badly need.
>
> Above all, we have to do our daily work. Whatever is good about the St. John's program — and *plenty* of it *is* good — can only show inasmuch as we apply ourselves seriously to our work, in seminars, laboratory, and tutorials. As to the deficiencies and shortcomings in the present set up, I feel confident that quite a few things can be straightened out, once we recover our balance. A great deal of preparatory work in this direction has actually been done by Mr. Wilburn. It will bear fruit.
>
> Let us not make the mistake of indulging in blind despair *or* in blind hope. It will all be pretty hard. But we are hardened too, it seems to me, aren't we?
>
> Have a good night.[1]

This short and simple speech was characteristic of Jacob Klein and indicated much about what his deanship would be like. It said what the occasion demanded, and, more than that, it placed squarely before the students and faculty what might seem like the obvious truth that the only way in which a college of liberal arts can achieve its goals, if it can, is through the daily work, what happens in the classroom from day to day. Klein, of course, knew that it was necessary from time to time both for students, as well as faculty, to stand back from their day-to-day work and reexamine the foundations and the plan of the program. But he also knew that endless uninformed criticism of what one is expected to do but isn't doing can be paralyzing with respect to learning. The practice of the liberal arts was more important than grandiose and empty talk about them. Klein did not pretend that everything about the St. John's program was good or promise that all its deficiencies would be eliminated. But there was plenty that was good and sufficient reason to hope that many things that were bad could be corrected. As he constantly did in the years that followed, he stressed the difficulty of the task. The difficulties inherent in the very high and possibly conflicting demands of the St. John's program, or of any decent liberal education, were something he never lost sight of. He himself had the courage to face the difficulties and not opt for easy superficial solutions, and he sought to awaken that courage in colleagues and students. He could recommend a good night's sleep as a necessary preliminary to summoning up one's courage.

Jacob Klein had been at St. John's for nearly eleven years. Before 1938 he had not heard of this tiny American college. Born in Libau, Russia, in 1899, he graduated from the Friedrichs Realgymnasium in Berlin in 1917, then studied philosophy, mathematics, and physics at the universities of Berlin and Marburg, where in 1922 he received his doctorate under the philosopher Nicolai Hartmann, who in 1933 wrote of the extraordinary value of Klein's participation in his seminars and of what he himself had learned from him. What was more important in his own education was the coming of Martin Heidegger to Marburg in 1925. Klein attended Heidegger's lectures regularly. Without being drawn to Heidegger's own philosophy, he could say of him that "he is the very great thinker of our time, although his moral qualities do not match his intellectual ones."[2] Klein's debt to Heidegger was well described by his friend Leo Strauss:

> Heidegger's work required and included what he called *Desdruktion* of the tradition. (Desdruktion is not quite so bad as destruction. It means taking down, the opposition of construction.) He intended to uproot Greek philosophy, especially Aristotle, but this presupposed the laying bare of the roots, the laying bare of it as it was in itself and not as it had come to apear

Jacob Klein.

in the light of tradition and of modern philosophy. Klein was more attracted by the Aristotle brought to light by Heidegger than by Heidegger's own philosophy.[3]

Later, on his own and without help from Heidegger, he turned to Plato. His study of Plato led him to the discovery that even if one learns much from the surface of a Platonic dialogue, one cannot get beyond the surface unless one sees the dialogue as a drama and becomes an actor in it. That is, the dialogue is written in such a way that the best reader will not get all that is intended unless he tests every argument, whether it be presented by Socrates or anyone else. He may have to produce some arguments of his own to counter those of Socrates or others. He must follow up every clue. This study of Aristotle and Plato had resulted in the conviction that, whatever course philosophizing might take, one thing necessary was a recovery of classical Greek philosophy.

Closely connected with the effort to recover classical philosophy was the one book he wrote before coming to the United States, *Die griechische Logistik und die Entstehung der Algebra* (published in 1934 and 1936), which has been translated into English by Eva Brann with the title *Greek Mathematical Thought and the Origin of Algebra*. This book shows the significance that numbers have in the philosophy of Plato and the revolution in the understanding of mathematics that came with the algebra of Viète and Descartes, and so brings to light the tremendous difference between ancient and modern mathematics and between ancient and modern ways of understanding in general. Otto Toeplitz said of this work, "Klein is not to be judged after the measure of a producing mathematician. He unites in happy degree mathematical knowledge and understanding with philosophic and philologic learning and a sense of history. . . . What he says is of quite different calibre from what is usually written on these questions."[4]

'In February 1937 Klein went to England to study certain manuscripts related to the history of mathematics and physics. While he was in England, it became apparent that a return to Germany would have meant for him certain death, since he was a Jew (descended from King David, so his grandmother said). There was a period of great anxiety when it was doubtful whether he could emigrate to the United States. Having finally received permission to come to the United States, he arrived on April 1, 1938. Through Paul Weiss, who was then at Bryn Mawr College, and Mortimer Adler he was brought into communication with Scott Buchanan. Buchanan saw at once that he was just the kind of person wanted and needed at St. John's. He was appointed for the 1938–39 session, the second year of the new program, the Emergency Committee in Aid of Displaced Scholars having made a small grant to pay his salary for that session.

On October 18, 1938, when he had been at the college only a few weeks,

he recorded his impressions in a letter to Else Tammann Husserl, who was subsequently to become Mrs. Klein:

> The experiment [he had hardly had time to learn that it was not to be called an experiment] as it is now seems to me all in all impossible. But things will straighten out in a couple of years. . . . The people of the New Program are without exception very nice and fanatically devoted (with reason) to the course. Barr, the President, and Buchanan, the Dean, are both first-rate teachers. Their seminar probably cannot be matched anywhere. The boys (of the New Program) are very good material. The fact is that it is almost unbelievable to me that all the things that occupied me for years, that is, the whole theme of my work, are realized here. The people don't do quite right, very much is superficial and they are not quite right about certain fundamentals. But it is exciting to see how over centuries and oceans unspoiled boys (most of them are) are impressed by Plato. They read with a directness that is sometimes frightening. . . . It is clear that I am in the right spot. . . . My duties are the following so far: (1) To check certain translations which the College is making because there are no English texts, for instance Ptolemy, Copernicus, Kepler, etc. — that is marvelous because I am learning so much. (2) To establish the curriculum of the third year (we are only in the second year). There will be great difficulties because the questions start here. (3) To read the Meno with teachers (later with the students too). (4) To work on my stuff without any obligations. You must admit: I could not have it better. I walked around the first days drunk with happiness. Somehow back in my mind I have a bad conscience when I think of all the things which are going on in Europe.[5]

Eleven years had passed since the writing of this letter and Klein as acting dean and then as dean found himself in the position of major responsibility for the curriculum that Buchanan had established. Convinced as he was of the fundamental rightness of that curriculum, he was not about to make any revolutionary changes. Precisely in that respect he was unlike Buchanan who, as Adler once said, thought that whatever has become established must have something wrong with it and who in 1943 had reported approvingly to his son Douglas the remark of a young faculty member that "almost everything has to be rebuilt if we are to go on." Klein certainly to a very large extent shared the opinions on which the St. John's program as Buchanan had envisaged it had been based; that the end of liberal education is the intellectual virtues and that the best way to develop and to cultivate

the intellectual virtues is through intensive acquaintance with the whole intellectual tradition of the Western World and through the liberal arts.

If we are to look for differences or disagreements with Buchanan, we shall have to infer them; for we shall not find Klein pointing them out. One place to look would be the dean's statement of educational policy and program, the first such statement as required by the polity that had been recommended by the faculty and adopted by the Board in 1950. After referring to the college catalogue, which was still largely as Buchanan had written it, as the basic statement of educational policy for the college, he listed three factors that are meant to regulate teaching and learning in every part of the program:
1. The community of the learning effort;
2. The continuity of the learning process;
3. The spontaneity of the learning itself.

As regards the community of the learning effort or the spontaneity of the learning itself, one finds nothing from which to conclude a difference between Buchanan and Klein. According to Klein, the community of the learning effort manifests itself (a) in the teacher's establishing a common ground with and among his students by a careful pondering of their thoughts, (b) in allowing the same subjects to come up for discussion in different classes and different contexts, and (c) in making the learning of the teachers a common enterprise both through their conversations with one another and their auditing the classes of other teachers. The spontaneity of learning, he asserted, requires (a) both routine work and an attitude of questioning and wondering that is related to the routine work, but goes beyond it, (b) both a sufficient amount of necessary work and sufficient leisure, and (c) both rigorous discipline and freedom. In all of this there was no departure from what Buchanan might have said.

But as concerns the second of the three factors listed there was a departure which had to do with what the continuity of the learning process means. Klein spoke of difficulties standing in the way of this continuity:

(a) Within the program there are certain large unities each of which depends upon a common subject matter such as whatever is common to great tragedies or the story of astronomy—partially but not entirely dialectical—that is implied in the names Ptolemy–Copernicus–Kepler–Newton. But also there are quite disparate subject matters which have to be approached in quite different ways and do not immediately reveal any unifying principles. Klein saw the continuity of learning at this point in the developing awareness among teachers and students of the difficulty of finding such principles and in the effort to overcome the difficulty. His earlier studies, before coming to St. John's, had revealed a gap, perhaps an unbridgeable chasm, between ancient thought and modern thought. He would have considered Buchanan's analogies as imaginative, but as presenting only a specious, and too easy, unity in the face of all the perplexities.

(b) The very wealth and comprehensiveness of the program in things to be learned mean that it necessitates hard work on the part of the student and the hard-working student may become so immersed in trying to grasp the content of this or that great book that he neglects to reflect upon the ways of thought and imagination that are involved in that effort. Klein thought an absorbing preoccupation with the content of a great book to be a necessary condition for learning. He did not think it sufficient. Buchanan was content if a student acquired only a superficial acquaintance with the content, provided that it were sufficiently suggestive and provocative of thought; if the thought moved far away from the book, that was no matter for concern.

(c) The third difficulty, according to Klein, arises in the attempt to find in the liberal arts a universal pattern for learning that is applicable to all subject matters. Of this pattern he said, "Its merits are unquestionable: it provides a network of references that seems to safeguard the continuity and unity of the learning process, without undue rigor and compulsion. Its defects are obvious: the vagueness and a certain artificiality in this kind of understanding of the liberal arts tend towards a sort of empty schematism and distract the attention of the students far too much from the content of their learning."[6]

There was a vagueness about Buchanan's doctrine that the proximate subject matters of all the liberal arts are first and second impositions and first and second intentions. Medieval logicians had spoken of the impositions and intentions under the general assumption that speaking and writing, and also thinking, are activities of signifying. First imposition means using a spoken or written word to signify a thing; second imposition means using such a word to signify itself as a word. If we speak or write: "A whale is a mammal," we are using the word "whale" to signify the animal. But if we say " 'whale' is a noun," we are using the same word to signify itself. The distinction between first intention and second intention is analogous, only it applies not to spoken or written signs, but to mental signs or concepts. A concept is used in first intention when it signifies a thing, in second intention when it signifies itself as a concept, as, for example, if we should think: " 'Whale' is a concept," referring to the mental sign corresponding to the word "whale." Unless Buchanan was using the impositions and intentions in quite a new and original way, which he did not make clear, while it is easy to see how certain of the traditional liberal arts might have as their proximate subject matters ways of using words or concepts, there does seem to be a certain vagueness in forcing the pattern of the liberal arts into union with this very special doctrine of signifying. Moreover, there was an artificiality in Buchanan's claim that music is "the art of measurement as we find it in the natural sciences" and that astronomy is "the study of functions and varients."

In pursuance of his desire that students should get a better grasp of the

content of the books and also have the leisure for reflection upon their reading, Klein began in some cases to reduce the number of pages read for seminar assignments and in other cases to distribute the reading over more seminars. For example: the last year Buchanan was dean the sophomores had one seminar on Genesis and Exodus together, one on Matthew and Mark together and one on Luke and John together, and one on Romans and First Corinthians, four in all. By the second year Klein was dean, they had two seminars on Genesis, one on Exodus, one on each of the gospels, one on Romans, and one on First and Second Corinthians, nine in all. Also in Buchanan's last year the sophomores read for their first seminar on Thomas Aquinas the first eight questions of the *Summa Theologiae* (I–I) and for their second seminar questions 9 through 13 of the same. In the second year of Klein's deanship the first seminar in Thomas Aquinas was devoted entirely to Question 1 on the nature and extent of sacred doctrine and the second seminar to question 2 containing the arguments for the existence of God and question 13 on the names of God. Whereas under Buchanan it was normal to read two plays of Shakespeare for one seminar, under Klein it became normal to read just one. In the junior year, the most notable reduction was in the readings from Kant's *Critique of Pure Reason*. Juniors reading certain passages judiciously selected were in a better position to understand Kant than earlier juniors who had sometimes read more than one hundred pages for a single seminar assignment. All this was a departure from Barr's original claim, that had also been made in the Virginia Report, that each book would be read in its entirety. Poetic works have, for the most part, been read in their entirety. So, as one would expect, have novels. No attempt was ever made to read all the propositions of Newton's *Principia;* that would have been folly. Newton himself says (Preface to Book III of the *Principia*) that "it is enough if one reads the Definitions, the Laws of Motion, and the first three sections of the first Book. He may then pass on to this Book and consult such of the remaining Propositions of the first Books, as the references in this and his occasions, shall require." The reduction in the amount of work done in seminar preparation as a consequence of Klein's policy was recognized by all as sheer gain, although it has seemed to many that the burden of work that is inherent in the St. John's program still makes it impossible to avoid altogether the second difficulty mentioned by Klein in connection with the continuity of the learning process.

One of the first new program students, one who went through four years of seminars with Buchanan as leader, has said of him that he thought that all young men were angels. Jacob Klein put it somewhat differently in a brief talk which was one of several delivered at a memorial service in Annapolis just after Buchanan's death: "The largeness and depth of his vision let him often overlook the foibles of those who were his students. He preferred to see in deficiencies the promises of further achievements rather than

irretrievable losses. That is to say, he understood the conditions for learning to be ever-present, the power of the intellect never entirely absent."[7]

We have already noted that, although the Virginia Report of 1935 envisaged an especially excellent kind of education for specially gifted students, Buchanan, by the time the program was instituted at St. John's, thought of it as a program not for the specially gifted, but for everyone of college age. Only if that were true, could he and Barr recommend it as a model for all American colleges to follow. Only if that were true, could it be the policy of St. John's to admit anyone who met the ordinary requirements for admission to college.

Klein in his second statement of educational policy and program which was adopted by the faculty on October 6, 1951, addressed himself to this policy:

> It has always been the policy of the College to allow for a very great latitude of aptitude and intelligence among its students. . . .
> Certain experiences seem to confirm the College's official position; other experiences seem to refute it. The College has had enough examples [i.e., enough to confirm its policy] of sudden awakenings, and radical changes in its students. It has also had enough examples [i.e., enough to call into question its policy] of persistent sleep. It is true that the College has contributed markedly to the intellectual development of some of its students. . . . On the other hand it is hard to deny that some seminars and tutorials suffer heavily from the activity, or rather inactivity, of vegetative or at best appetitive souls.

He went on to refer to certain measures taken by the Instruction Committee to benefit the less gifted student without hindering the progress of the more gifted ones, measures, he emphasized, not meant to curtail in any student freedom and spontaneity of learning.

Klein was not going to change the admissions policy of the college. He was not going to select from all applicants especially intelligent students or students deemed especially fit for the St. John's kind of education. Like Buchanan he believed in the power of the intellect. He was, nevertheless, more aware than Buchanan was of the obstacles that tend to nullify the conditions of learning, obstacles that arise because of man's vegetative or appetitive nature. It is unlikely that he would ever have had the dream that Buchanan had that every man could be a Socrates to another man.

This dream had something to do with Buchanan's minimizing the role of those who were technically called teachers or the St. John's faculty. Klein, it seems, although he never made a point of this as a difference between

him and Buchanan, believed that the success of the program depended in large measure upon the faculty. The importance of a first-rate faculty was something he stressed persistently in his reports to the board. In his report to the board in November of the year in which he became dean, he stated that to him the most important problem was that of the faculty, and he proceeded to rank the twenty-eight members of the faculty without naming them individually as ten first-rate, six not bad but second-rate, five of questionable teaching ability, and seven somewhere between the second-rate and the questionable. It is highly doubtful whether Buchanan would ever have made such a ranking, which does not mean that he thought all the St. John's faculty were first-rate teachers, being first-rate learners.

During Klein's deanship the college, with a grant from the Ford Foundation, engaged in a self-study project under the direction of Clarence J. Kramer of the class of 1946, who later became the first dean of St. John's second campus in Santa Fe, New Mexico. The project included several enterprises, among them a conference in 1953 on the program in which conference the participants were eight members of the St. John's faculty together with about twice as many educators from elsewhere. Klein was the chairman and moderator for the meetings. Buchanan was one of the participants. At the last of the meetings the following exchange occurred between the two:

> *Buchanan*: I am sure some of you know that in the early days, when we were trying to formulate this program, we were concerned about the whole range of virtues, and the theological virtues were seriously inquired into. There was a concern about Faith, Hope, and Charity. . . .
> When I visit academic institutions these days it seems there is a dismal grim dullness about everything because everyone is afraid he might have an ideology, faith or something or other. The intellect does not live without this, without faith, without something of the sort. . . . We have to have something that will bring the intellect back to life. I have not any solution for this.
> *Klein*: The intellect lives.
> *Buchanan*: Yes, it does. But the intellect if it lives produces or flowers in a faith, and we do not know how to discuss that.
> *Klein*: That is not discussable.[8]

As the meeting proceeded, Edwin Garlan of Reed College expressed the opinion that good colleges, when successful in inculcating the intellectual virtues, were at the same time sadly failing by causing a turning away from life, and, in connection with Buchanan's remarks, suggested that this was due to a "lack of faith, a lack of a sense of direction, of purpose within action." "It seems," he said, "you do not need an ideology to cultivate the in-

tellectual virtues; but perhaps you need one to give that product its full flowering in action."

Klein replied: "Mr. Buchanan, I am sure, has a different kind of answer to that. My answer to your problem is a very simple one. Proposition 1: I believe there is nothing higher than intellectual activity. Proposition 2: This is not the common activity of men. Proposition 3: The normal thing that happens is a turning toward life. Proposition 4: The greater the preceding intellectual activity, the better the turning will be."

This interchange makes more explicit the differences between Buchanan and Klein. Klein, while not being an adherent of any religion, was more aware than most Jews or Christians of what it means to be the one or the other. Such was his concern that Jewish students be familiar with their great heritage that he was largely instrumental in bringing on the faculty Simon Kaplan, who for more than thirty years conducted an extracurricular class in the Hebrew Bible, interpreting it from the point of view of the Jewish tradition. It was Klein's habit not to judge the truth or falsity of any proposition made within the horizon of revealed religion on the ground that such a judgment could not be made without faith. Statements of faith were in that sense for him not discussable outside of faith, except insofar as the intellect might explicate the meaning of those statements without judging truth or falsity. Hence he could not subscribe to Buchanan's urging the need of faith *as an imperative* for bringing the intellect to life. Buchanan was surely more extreme than the theologians. Thomas Aquinas no doubt would have said that revealed truths, received in faith, give to the intellect the possibilty of a vastly greater life of contemplation than it would otherwise have; he would not have said that the intellect is dead without faith. But did Buchanan really mean that it was dead? He immediately assented to Klein's simple declaration: "The intellect lives." Would an ideology, or something else, be the equivalent of faith? In any case, were the doctrines of faith for Buchanan more than material for lively intellectual gymnastics? He frequently said that belief in the Incarnation was not the main thing, but rather belief in the possibility of the Incarnation. Garlan, in picking up Buchanan's point, was really saying something quite different. Instead of seeing faith or an ideology as the flowering of the intellectual virtues as such, he was seeing faith or an ideology as producing a flowering of the intellectual virtues in life by which he meant action.

The intellect lives, said Klein. One might say that for him that was the basic assumption of St. John's College. The intellectual life, a life lived in single-minded pursuit of truth, was the highest life. That was not, he said, and it is hard to see how it can be, the life that most human beings live. Yet insofar as their lives could be directed or even to some degree moved by the intellect, they would be better lives. Action without the guidance of reason was, according to him, not genuine action.

Klein's greatest contribution to the College as dean may have been his own way of leading the intellectual life. As he had said of Barr and Buchanan, and of ten others, he himself was a first-rate teacher. He and Buchanan used to accuse one another of mesmerizing students. They were both right. But the word "accuse" may not be appropriate. The real meaning of the "mesmerizing" was that both had inimitable ways of winning and holding the attention of students, of getting students fascinated in considering and exploring important questions. Klein, more than Buchanan, voiced his own opinions in seminar discussions but in such a way as not to hinder contrary opinions from having a fair go in the argument. His deep concern to recover an understanding of the ancient classical philosophy never had a doctrinaire character and never led him to try to make of St. John's a Platonic or Aristotelian academy. The spontaneity of a student's learning was treasured by him in deed as well as speech.

Through his lectures Klein not only gave splendid examples of the liberal arts in action but also helped many teachers and students in the common effort to understand the great books. There was a wide range of subject matter to which he devoted careful attention and hard work. Besides lectures on the liberal arts, which it had become the custom for the dean to give annually, and lectures on Plato and Aristotle, there were lectures on "The Problem and Art of Writing," a large part of which dealt with Homer's *Iliad;* on Virgil; on Dante's *Purgatorio*; on the Copernican innovation; on Descartes; on Leibniz's thought as a whole; on Kant's thought as a whole; on "The Nineteenth Century." The lecture on the nineteenth century had to do with Hegel and such post-Hegelians as Marx, Kierkegaard, and Nietzsche. He was fascinated by the letters of Paul the apostle and was once thinking of giving a lecture on Paul. That he did not was due no doubt to his sensitivity to the feelings and opinions of other Jews. All of Klein's lectures contained something solid, something one would want to ponder. All merit reading and rereading.

CHAPTER 9

A Time of Stabilization and Deeper Understanding

The nine years between 1949 and 1958, at the beginning of Wiegle's long tenure as president of the college and during which Klein was dean, were years of stabilization and deeper understanding of the aims and content of the St. John's program. Weigle's efforts resulted in greater financial stability. Their joint efforts resulted in increased enrollment. Klein did much to improve the quality of the faculty, and while performing arduous administrative duties, he continued to lead the faculty and students in the work and play of learning.

Klein's reports to the Board during the nine years that he was dean show what were principal matters of concern to him: (1) the decline in the number of students enrolled; (2) obtaining and training new faculty members; and, above all, (3) maintaining and improving the curriculum.

In spite of the decline in the enrollment during the first five years of his term in office he remained optimistic, and the events proved his optimism to be justified. For the enrollment gradually but steadily increased during the last four years he was dean and continued to increase until at mid-year in the session of 1958–59 there were 192 students.[1] By 1960 there were 277,[2] and the president of the college could now reasonably suggest setting as a goal a maximum enrollment of 400. For this suggestion he was burned in effigy in November 1960 by a few students who thought that such a huge number would destroy the unity of the college as an intimate community of learning.

At the board meeting in May 1949[3] Klein announced that the faculty would be strengthened in the following year by the return of Richard Scofield, who had been at the University of Chicago on leave of absence, and by the addition of William A. Darkey, an alumnus of the class of 1942 who had recently completed a course of graduate study at Columbia and was later to be the second dean of St. John's in Santa Fe. Klein's continued concern with the quality of the faculty was shown when, at a board meeting in the spring of 1950,[4] he emphasized the quite special demands made upon every

M. E. Warren

Richard D. Weigle.

member of the St. John's faculty by a program in which the teacher has to seek to acquire a more than superficial understanding of all that is taught. In September of the same year[5] he stated that the biggest task was to obtain faculty of high quality. In 1955[6], while noting improvement, he was still saying to the board that one great problem to be solved was that of obtaining a competent faculty.

There were certain steps that Klein took to develop a better faculty. One was the institution of teaching internships made possible in 1953 by a grant from the Ford Foundation. The interns were young men and women who had completed some graduate study and who were to come to St. John's to spend a year in which they would acquire some knowledge of the program and engage in a certain amount of teaching with a view possibly to becoming permanent members of the faculty. It was also expected that the internship program would relieve members of the faculty of some of the burdens of an arduous teaching assignment. Seven interns were appointed for the first year, six of whom were supported by the grant from the Ford Foundation. Originally the grant was for just one year but the Foundation continued to support the internships through the academic session of 1956-57. Unfortunately, there were no more after that because the college had no funds of its own for their continuance. It was unfortunate that they were discontinued, because the internship program was a way in which the college added several valuable members to its faculty, and all of the interns, including those who did not become members of the faculty, agreed that they had benefitted from participating in the St. John's program.

Another measure taken by Klein to improve the faculty was the establishment of faculty study groups. There is little danger that the St. John's faculty member will grow stale, since he or she is constantly moving on within the curriculum to learn and to teach new things, and even when there is a return to teaching Sophocles or Euclid or Newton, it is very likely to be after one has taught Shakespeare or Lobachevski or Einstein, and the old things are seen in a new light and provoke a new wonder. Nevertheless, however great its scope, the program, because of the amount of work involved, has often prevented faculty members from studying things outside of but relevant to it, or from studying more deeply what is included in it. It was to provide for these kinds of study that Klein in the session of 1956-57[7] instituted the first faculty study group. This group, on a reduced teaching assignment, studied Mathematical Logic under the chairmanship of Curtis Wilson, who later succeeded Klein as dean. Willard V. Quine, professor of philosophy at Harvard, was invited to spend a week with the group so that they could profit from his extensive knowledge of Mathematical Logic. The faculty study groups have continued up to the present and have dealt with such subjects as Poetics, Thermodynamics, Hegel's *Phenomenology of Spirit,* General Relativity, and the Logic of William of Ockham, to name only a few.

In his brief speech to the faculty and students in January 1949 when he became acting dean, Klein referred to the preparatory work already begun by Wilburn to correct deficiencies in the curriculum. Wilburn had, among other things, encouraged a committee of intelligent and responsible students[8] to undertake a study of the laboratory. The committee made their report in 1948. It was their opinion that the laboratory had, during the first ten years of the program, failed in its purpose, if indeed its purpose had ever been clearly defined. They assumed that the original intention when the St. John's program was started was that the Cartesian revolution in mathematics and natural science should be a major focus for the laboratory.

We should note, however, that Buchanan neither in the Virginia Report of 1935 nor in the first catalogue statement of the program made any mention of the Cartesian revolution. Buchanan had in mind, as has been said, three kinds of laboratories: (1) a measurement laboratory in which the students would become familiar with the basic instruments of measurement, the quantities they measure, and the ways they measure them; (2) a laboratory that would repeat crucial experiments in historic and contemporary science, experiments such as Galileo's with the inclined plane; and (3) a laboratory to combine scientific findings in the investigation of concrete problems. He saw this kind of laboratory as concerned with problems of biological or medical science.

In the catalogue statement for 1938–39, the second one, which also came from Buchanan's pen, there was mention for the first time of the Cartesian revolution which was said to be "perhaps the greatest intellectual revolution in recorded history." "Descartes," it was said, "by using and interpreting the knowledge of the Greeks, made modern mathematics and the laboratory possible so that now if we would follow the classical thread into the modern world we must know the constructions of the mathematicians and find our classical loci in the instruments of the laboratory as well as in the great books."[9] It may be that the emphasis on the Cartesian revolution had resulted from conversation between Buchanan and Klein who was particularly insistent on the revolutionary consequences for all of modern thought of Descartes' way of thinking. Be that as it may, Buchanan saw no reason that focusing on the Cartesian revolution should alter his threefold plan for the laboratory.

Returning to the work of the student committee who had been attempting to find what had been supposed to be the guiding principles for the laboratory up to 1948, we find the following statements:

1. (The laboratory) is to be conceived as a whole and not as a group of disparate subject matters, e.g., as a course in physics, a course in biology, and a course in chemistry. . . .
2. It exists in a context—the rest of the program. This would immediately seem to subject it to certain limitations so far as ordering is

concerned. The ordering would have to parallel the seminar and tutorial work were the context not to be disrupted.
3. Observations and operations are means, not the end. A liberalized and humanized science would declare that the mind of man must rule his techniques and must not be ruled by them; that 'understandings' and 'insights' are more needed than an accumulation of scientific information.
4. Professional schools and their requirements are not to dictate the organization of the laboratory. It is an instrument of liberation and it is good to the degree that it serves that purpose. It is necessary in a liberal arts program because it is desirable that man arrive at an understanding of his world, his civilization, to live well. We in our western world are faced with the critical problem of understanding and assimilating the great intellectual revolution of the 17th century. This is one of the ends of the laboratory along with the rest of the program.
5. The laboratory is dialectical. Its form is not a question of dogma.[10]

The committee thought that these principles that were supposed to have served as a guide for the laboratory had never actually done so, that there had never been an overall plan, and that the attempts to correlate the sciences with one another and the rest of the program had been sporadic, fragmentary, and unsuccessful. While they declared that they had rather be caught dead than recommend a grand synthesis, they deplored what they thought to be the course the college had taken in abandoning all attempts at correlation and falling back into the conventional pattern of teaching physics, chemistry, and biology, as separate enterprises, a pattern they considered to be essentially incoherent.

They recommended what they called an organic laboratory by which they would bring the laboratory into an organic relationship with the rest of the curriculum by using it to investigate, by means of experiment, observation, and measurement, certain ideas that would be formulated in advance and would have a clear relevance to other parts of the program, and some of which could be as relevant to the reading of ancient texts as others would be to the reading of modern texts. They mentioned Time, Space, Structure, Function, Attraction, Element, Nature, and others. They conceded the enormous difficulty of such an enterprise, but thought it possible if a special committee were given the leisure to "devise and revise." The committee would consist of St. John's faculty, graduates, and others. It would include both professional scientists and philosophers.

It is not surprising that the committee found that there are "almost insuperable obstacles" to the effort to set up and maintain a laboratory in accordance with the principles they formulated. Nor is it surprising that they found that the St. John's laboratory had failed.

First, while there have been wonderful feats of unifying achieved by a Newton, a Clark Maxwell, or an Einstein, or in Biology through Darwin's evolutionary account, it is a question of whether modern science exists as one whole rather than many disparate wholes. Second, if the laboratory is to be correlated throughout with the seminar, the question inevitably arises what experiments or measurements in the laboratory might accompany, in such a way as to be fruitful in "understandings" and "insights," the study of the Greek poets, Plato, Aristotle, Lucretius, the Bible, Dante, Chaucer, and Shakespeare, the authors or books that provide the principal basis for the seminar discussions of the first two years. If one begins the study of modern science in those years, can one relate it in more than a superficial way to those discussions? On the other hand, if one postpones the study of modern science to the last two years of a four-year college curriculum, can one do so without crowding so much into those years that there is no room for the leisurely reflection without which nothing is really learned? Third, there is, in any kind of organized education, whether it be the St. John's kind or not, the danger of becoming so absorbed in acquiring the means of learning that one loses sight of the ends. Fourth, since many students in liberal arts colleges go on to graduate or professional schools, such colleges inevitably feel a certain pressure to ignore the ends of liberal education and to provide what is needed as preparation for a study that is directed toward a career. Finally, it is more difficult to preserve a dialectic with respect to the presuppositions of the sciences, to question them in a sustained and meaningful way, than it is simply to accept them and the systematic consequences that follow. Even in the sciences generally accepted opinions become dogmas.

The committee's proposal for an "organic" laboratory based on the investigation of certain terms that would provide links with the seminar discussions was perhaps impracticable. Jacob Klein did not attempt to put that proposal into effect. Instead, he continued the practice of teaching biology, chemistry, and physics more or less separately, but with full recognition of the principles that the student committee had so well formulated and that all along had been supposed to guide the laboratory. During Klein's deanship there were in the first two years of the laboratory observations and experiments that were relatively simple, and that did not require modern mathematics. In the last two years students encountered Newtonian mechanics and electromagnetism. To get a good grasp of these was made difficult by the fact that it was only in the senior year in their mathematics tutorial that they began to study the differential and integral calculus. It was not until after Klein's term as dean that the calculus was moved to the junior year of the mathematics tutorial with the obvious consequent benefit to the laboratory. At a board meeting in December 1952, Klein reported that the laboratory was working better and that the physics and biology were being well handled.[11] He certainly did not at any time during his deanship

think that the problems involved in teaching modern sciences in the St. John's laboratory and within the context of the whole curriculum had been solved.

At the conference held in the autumn of 1953 in connection with the self-study project, one session was devoted to the role of science in a liberal arts curriculum. St. John's faculty took part in the discussion as well as educators from outside the college, including Scott Buchanan. Buchanan insisted that, although in the first ten years of the program the problem of the unity of the sciences (i.e., the problem of discovering that and how the several sciences are one science) had not been cracked, it was imperative for the college to crack it or else have its liberal program smashed by the technical orientation of the sciences. Klein agreed about the seriousness of the problem and the necessity of trying to deal with it. But he did not see the lack of unity in the sciences as the principal enemy.

"The enemy," he said, "is the matter-of-course attitude toward science, namely the taking for granted that there is such a thing and that whatever is unclear about it will be clarified. That, I think, is the enemy. . . . the only unity that matters in the context of a liberal arts college and the context of education is that there is an increase in the powers of our understanding in dealing with any single matter. That alone, it seems to me, justifies the enterprise. . . . the problem of unity is the problem of the sciences and all the other fields of learning. There, it seems to me, it is very hard even to postulate unity. I am not saying that we should not envisage the possibility and even seek it, and even be aware that we actually proceed under this assumption; but I am not sure whether this would actually help us do the job properly."[12]

The St. John's faculty present at this conference seemed to agree with Klein that it would not help to impose a hypothetical unity upon the modern natural sciences, and that if a unity of the sciences were to be found, it could only be through a prior thoroughgoing examination of the foundations of the sciences as they exist.

There were few changes in the language tutorial while Jacob Klein was dean. Latin had been dropped while Wilburn was dean in favor of two years of Greek, one year of German, and one year of French. In 1962 German was to be dropped in favor of two years of French. The reason for dropping German was very much the same as the reason for dropping Latin earlier. Though acquiring anything like a mastery of the particular language was never the object of the language tutorial, it was thought that knowledge of a particular language that was more than a smattering was necessary for investigating the nature of language as embodying thought. It is true that during Klein's deanship what had started as a second year of Greek came to be roughly a half-year of Greek and a half-year of English.

Klein always distinguished between music and the fine arts. He considered the study of music to be the study of rhetoric in its purest form and as deserving a place within a liberal arts curriculum because of maintain-

ing, not as is so often said, a balance between the intellect and emotions, but a balance within the intellectual life itself. He therefore encouraged the expansion of the music program which occurred under Victor Zuckerkandl. Klein was never convinced that works of painting, sculpture, and architecture have the intellectual content that would make them worthy of study within a liberal arts curriculum. At the same time he believed that the college should provide the opportunity for students to engage in painting and sculpting as extracurricular activities.

It had been Buchanan's hope and expectation that the seminar discussions would bring to life a conversation among the doctrines and arguments presented in the great books. Such a conversation can be brought to life, however, only if the students remember and can articulate with some clarity those doctrines and arguments as they move on through the program. All too often it had happened that students in their third and fourth years had only a vague memory of what they had read in the first year. An effort to correct this situation was made when Wilburn was dean. During the academic session of 1948–49 the seniors had seminar discussions not only on nineteenth and twentieth century books, but on Plato's *Theaetetus, Philebus, Parmenides, Sophist,* and *Statesman* as well as selections from Aristotle's *De Anima* and *Metaphysics*. This effort was continued in a diminished way while Jacob Klein was dean. In the sessions of 1949–50 and 1950–51 the seniors read Plato's *Sophist* and Books VII and XII of Aristotle's *Metaphysics*. The *Sophist* continued to be read for the senior seminars all the time that Klein was dean, though Aristotle's *Nicomachean Ethics* came to be substituted for the selections from the *Metaphysics*.

It has been generally conceded by those planning changes in the St. John's curriculum that it is more difficult to decide what nineteenth and twentieth century books are of lasting significance than it is to decide about earlier books. For this reason there have been more changes in the senior seminar reading list than in the seminar reading lists for the other years. Tolstoi's *War and Peace* and a large number of readings from Hegel and Marx's *Capital* have been almost always present on the senior list, while readings from Pierce, James, Whitehead, Dewey, and Wittgenstein have come and gone. Klein introduced Kierkegaard and Nietzsche to the senior list, and they seem to have attained a certain permanence following Hegel and Marx. Klein also introduced readings related to American political institutions and American political and economic problems. Readings of this kind have continued up to the present to be the principal material for seminar discussions among the seniors during their last few weeks before graduation.

In presenting the plan for such readings Klein stated:

> The Faculty will have to consider the selections already made or envisaged for the future very carefully. It has to avoid, with

all the circumspection at its command, two pitfalls. It should not give emphasis to the superficial discussions of current political problems which reflect, perhaps more than anything else, the deplorable infantilism of contemporary life and thus increase the reigning immaturity in judgement and action. And it cannot rely on the existing social sciences with their unquestioned and yet highly questionable methodology and terminology borrowed from the natural sciences. Like any other material chosen for the nourishment of the learning mind, this one, [i.e., material relating to American political and economic problems], presenting basic issues within an industrialized and global civilization, must be seen in the light of the traditional crucial problems which man cannot avoid facing at all times and which, in fact, form the texture of the great books throughout the four years.[13]

It has been the experience of many students at St. John's that the rapid pace at which they study the great books has hindered them from gaining the thorough understanding they desire. The rightness of this desire, long recognized by the faculty, led in 1960-61 to the institution of the preceptorials under Curtis Wilson, Klein's successor. The preceptorials enabled juniors and seniors to study certain books or subjects with a care and intensity that they were unable to give to ordinary seminar assignments. This necessitated the elimination of many seminars with a consequent reduction in the seminar reading list; the effort to have all the seniors recover or acquire an understanding of Plato and Aristotle to put in a dialectical relationship to an understanding of Hegel, Marx, etc., was henceforth abandoned.

One of the persistent criticisms made of the St. John's curriculum has been that the study of history is neglected. Jacob Klein all during his deanship had always defended that neglect on the ground that, given the present prejudices in academic institutions, the study of history can easily lead to the assumption that the necessary and sufficient way to understand human thought, actions, and institutions is historical. He thought that the assumption that all things fall into an essentially historical pattern inevitably presents an obstacle to raising and confronting the simple question of the truth or falsity of the thought of an Aristotle or a Lucretius or a Kant. Most of the faculty have agreed with Klein and there has never been any endeavour to incorporate within the curriculum a study of history or a study of the "historical background" of the great books. Occasionally, this neglect has caused a failure to understand certain things for which a knowledge of something that happened in the past is indeed relevant. To be sure, to a large extent, since the books are read more or less in chronological order, the earlier books provide a context for the later books.

It was under Jacob Klein that the self-study project already mentioned was undertaken. St. John's, while having defined for itself with some clarity the ends and to a considerable extent the means of liberal education, has constantly recognized the necessity of asking where and why it might have failed in making clear the ends, in directing the students towards the ends, in providing them with the means. The self-study project was begun in 1953 and conducted by Clarence J. Kramer, having been made possible by a grant from the Ford Foundation. As part of the project, Kramer sent out a questionnaire to all alumni who had been through the program. A brief summary of the replies may help to give a picture of the college's program in the eyes of the alumni up to the middle of Jacob Klein's tenure as dean.

The overwhelming number (121 out of 144) were enthusiastic about the kind of education they received. In general they found the seminar the most successful part and the laboratory the least successful part of the program. When asked how the seminars might be improved, they were on the whole reluctant to prescribe rules, but there were suggestions that there might be better seminar leaders, that the seminar leaders might take a more active role in discussions, that thoughtful reading in preparation for discussions might require reducing the amount of material read. Criticisms of the laboratory were that it was "spotty and uneven, neither consistently good nor consistently bad," that it was disorganized, that the repetition of experiments crucial in the past for the verification of an hypothesis or the discovery of a law gave the students little understanding of the "scientific method." While some of the alumni thought that the teachers, when leading seminars, might take a more active role, in general they approved of the St. John's view that the role of the teacher is to lead the students in a common inquiry. Consequently they, for the most part, saw no reason for the tutors to be more authoritative. They likened the tutors to guides. One of the alumni, elaborating on this point said, "A good guide, in interesting terrain, will suggest new and rewarding paths of exploration; his advice is always valuable. A poor guide is more a hindrance than a help. But a guide, good or poor, remains always a means and never the end. The terrain is the final master; it alone, not the guide, has concealed secrets." Nearly all the alumni praised the St. John's program for its breadth at the same time that they regretted that this breadth itself made it difficult for the student to attain excellence through a thorough investigation of a subject. In response to the question how the St. John's program compared with that of other colleges with which the alumni might be familiar, an alumnus who had become a college professor said, "It produces less of a sense and ability of craft and workmanship, less of a respect for professional skill, but more of an individual sense of intellectual effort and responsibility. That is, it makes imaginative thinkers who do their own thinking, are not stultified by author-

ity, but it can also make loose, often pretentious talkers who think knowledge comes easier than it does."[14]

It has already been noted[15] that Klein, in his first statement of educational policy in 1950, both commended the attempt that had been made by Buchanan to find in the seven liberal arts a universal pattern for "tying together dissimilar or conflicting disciplines," and observed that the liberal arts employed as an empty schematism might distract the student from the content of his learning. During the whole course of his deanship he raised and reraised the question of the liberal arts and sought to find different ways of saying what they are or are not. His starting point was the common understanding that the liberal arts are arts that are intended to make men free, freedom being not simply freedom from external compulsion but freedom from the tyranny of passions and prejudices, freedom from accepted opinions and conventional views, freedom for a life according to reason, or for the pursuit of learning for its own sake.

The original conception of the liberal arts, according to Klein, was based on the assumption that there are things that can be learned and therefore known and that, for that reason, the original liberal arts were the mathematical arts of the quadrivium: arithmetic, geometry, astronomy, and harmonics. These arts, it seemed, led to knowledge of numbers and figures and their relationships whether as unchanging or in motion. In addiiton, Klein claimed, there was a fifth liberal art, the inquiry concerning nature referred to by Socrates in Plato's *Phaedo* and by Aristotle in his reference to "the investigation of nature." In time questions arose about the ultimate foundations of these arts, about whether they could strictly be considered to be knowledge, about the possibility that, whatever aid they might give the understanding in its pursuit of truth, they might restrict it. A deeper and wider investigation was required, the depth and breadth of which might be found in human speech. Thus the arts of the trivium — grammar, rhetoric, and logic — came to be added. They are embodied in all human speech. One becomes aware of them as arts when reflection upon the forms embodied in speech makes it possible to separate and identify the different forms and to discern the role they play in questioning and learning. The arts of the trivium as such are a necessary means to that freedom toward which a liberal education is directed. They contain no guarantee of that freedom.

According to Klein, great changes occurred in the last four hundred years in the very understanding of the liberal arts. The arts of the quadrivium, arithmetic, geometry, astronomy, and harmonics (as distinguished from music), and the inquiry concerning nature had merged in one huge art called mathematical physics with biology not as a separate art, but as an ancillary discipline. The connection between the love of speech and the love of wisdom to be found sometimes in the ancient practice of the arts of the trivium had been very nearly lost with only the love of speech or "appreciation of

literature" remaining. The art of logic, too, had become divorced from the quest for wisdom and had either become a partner of mathematics or had usurped the place of philosophy.

Klein proposed two rules to observe in considering both the ancient practice of the liberal arts and the transformations in form and content that they have undergone in modern times. The first rule was to engage in philosophical reflection upon the presuppositions underlying the ways the liberal arts present things, the technical notions that govern that presentation, and the content that is presented. The second rule was to counteract the process of what he called "sedimentation" and to find the right ways to do that.

The term "sedimentation" and the thought behind it Klein owed to Edmund Husserl. "According to him (Husserl)," Klein said in a lecture given at St. John's, "the signifying power of a word has, by its very nature, the tendency to lose its revealing character. The more we become accustomed to words, the less we perceive their original and precise significance; a kind of superficial and vague understanding is the necessary result of the increasing familiarity with spoken and written words. Yet that original significance is still there, in every word, somehow 'forgotten,' but still at the bottom of our speaking and understanding, however vague the meaning conveyed by our speech might be. The original 'evidence' has faded away, but has not disappeared completely. It need not be 'awakened' even, it underlies our mutual understanding in a 'sedimented' form. 'Sedimentation is always somehow forgetfulness . . . ' And this kind of forgetfulness accompanies, of necessity, according to Husserl, the development and growth of any science."[16]

In February 1958 Jacob Klein, believing that nine years was long enough for anyone to serve as dean, resigned that office. He had been a wise guardian and critic of the curriculum. Upon the occasion of his resignation, Richard Weigle, the president of the college, acknowledged his debt to Klein for "new insights into liberal education."[17] The board expressed their appreciation of his service: "We know him to be a man of learning with the sensitivity and wit to make the power and beauty of knowledge the recognizable goals of those whose education is in his charge."[18] Klein responded by saying that "nothing in his life had been so important as the years spent at St. John's."[19] He continued as a member of the faculty and now had time to write two books, a commentary on Plato's *Meno* and *Plato's Trilogy*, an exegisis of Plato's *Theaetetus*, *Sophist*, and *Statesman*.

The resignation of Klein was in many ways the end of an era. Buchanan and Klein had, each of them, held the office of Dean for nine years. Each of them had an authority that was acknowledged by practically everyone within the college and that depended more upon what they were in themselves than upon powers conferred on them by the office. Buchanan,

more than anyone else, deserves to be called the founder of the program. Klein did a very great work in getting it firmly established and in leading those involved in it to a clearer and deeper understanding of it. At the time of his resignation the enrollment was on the increase, many excellent new members had been added to the faculty, and definite improvements, though no substantial changes, had been made in the curriculum.

The good estate of the college made it possible for Richard Weigle, who had already done so much to obtain needed buildings and endowment, to dream of expanding St. John's, not by increasing the size of the college in Annapolis, but by establishing other campuses of the same institution. On December 26, 1960, the news magazine *Time* contained the following news: "Though U.S. big-name colleges are deluged with applicants, most of them, fearing loss of quality in size, refuse to expand. One alternative is to start affiliates in distant places—a Yale-in-Denver, a Harvard-in-Dallas."

"Last week St. John's College showed the way. Richard D. Weigle invaded Manhattan to find foundation cash for his venture. St. John's aims to reproduce itself in as many as six affiliates across the country, starting with a new St. John's in California. The California affiliate will probably open in 1964 and will eventually become independent. Long before then, St. John's hopes to be spawning other affiliates in other parts of the country."

This "news" contained a kernel of truth. For St. John's College, having received in 1962 a handsome gift of land in Santa Fe, New Mexico, from John and Faith Meen, established there a second campus which came into being principally through the energy and devotion of Richard Weigle and which opened for students in the autumn of 1964. The arrangement for the two campuses was such that there were to be one president and one board for both and a joint instruction committee to ensure the continuance of the program in both places.

It is beyond the intention of this narrative to tell the story of the college since the Santa Fe campus came into being. In both places the St. John's program, in spite of being constantly subjected to reexamination and in spite of many interesting and significant changes, has remained in all its most fundamental aspects what it was as conceived by Buchanan and instituted by Barr and Buchanan in 1937. There is a strong loyalty to this program on the part of the faculty, students, and alumni. Along with this loyalty goes the recognition, especially well articulated by Jacob Klein, that the very institutionalization of liberal education contains a threat to liberal education. An educational institution has to devise curriculums, set courses, give examinations, assign grades, award degrees. Yet all these things may, and often do, make the student serve a kind of routine that inhibits the spontaneity of learning. Moreover, an educational institution, by its very nature, is concerned with the passing on of a tradition. Yet in the passing on of a tradition there may well occur, not so much the loss, as the concealment

or the blurring of the insights that are at the roots of the tradition — what Jacob Klein described as sedimentation. This is as true of the tradition embodied in great books as of any other. Finally, any educational institution owes its existence to a larger whole, a political community and a public, and therefore has an obligation to that community and that public. Yet the very demands that are thereby put upon it may hinder it from a fair and full assessment or criticism of those demands and from the pursuit of its higher goals. The sobering recognition of these dangers, while it almost certainly will not enable St. John's College to avoid them altogether, may nonetheless help it in the performance of its task of freeing the human intellect.

Appendix

1938–1939

Year	Language and Literature	Liberal Arts	Mathematics and Science
FIRST	Homer Herodotus Thucydides Aeschylus Sophocles Euripides Aristophanes Plutarch Lucian	Plato Aristotle Lucretius	Euclid Hippocrates Nichomachus Aristarchus Archimedes
SECOND	Tacitus Virgil *The Bible* Justinian Dante Saga of Burnt Njal Song of Roland Chaucer Villon Cervantes	Cicero Plotinus Augustine Scotus Erigena Bonaventura Thomas Aquinas Grosseteste Nicholas of Cusa	Apollonius Ptolemy Galen Leonardo Copernicus Galileo Descartes Gilbert
THIRD	Shakespeare Milton Rabelais Corneille Racine Molière Erasmus Montaigne Machiavelli Pascal Montesquieu Grotius Fielding Gibbon Voltaire Swift	Calvin Spinoza Francis Bacon Hobbes Locke Hume Kant Peacock Boole	Kepler Harvey Newton Leibniz Boyle Huygens Lavoisier Dalton
FOURTH	Goethe Rousseau Adam Smith American *Constitution* Federalist Papers Malthus Marx Zola Balzac Flaubert Thackery Dickens Ibsen Dostoevski Tolstoi	Schopenhauer Hagel Bentham Mill James Freud Poincaré Hilbert Russell	Fourier Hamilton Faraday Joule Ostwald Darwin Virchow Bernard Galton Mendel Cantor Dedekind Riemann Lobachevski Veblen & Young

Appendix

1982–1983

Literature	Philosophy and Theology	History and Social Science	Mathematics and Natural Science		Music
Homer Aeschylus Sophocles Euripides Aristophanes	Plato Aristotle Lucretius	Herodotus Thucydides Plutarch	Euclid Nicomachus Ptolemy Lavoisier Dalton Lamarck Archimedes Torricelli Pascal Fahrenheit Avogadro Black	Wollaston Gay-Lussac Proust Cannizzaro Berthollet T. Richter Thomson Berzelius Dulong Harvey Galen	
Virgil Dante Chaucer Rabelais Shakespeare Donne Marvell	Aristotle Epictetus Plotinus Marcus Aurelius *The Bible* Augustine Anselm Thomas Aquinas Luther Montaigne Bacon	Plutarch Tacitus Machiavelli	Ptolemy Apollonius Copernicus Descartes Darwin Mendel Pascal Viète		Palestrina Bach Mozart Beethoven Schubert Stravinsky Haydn Des Prez Webern
Cervantes Milton Swift Racine Fielding Melville La Fontaine Wordsworth Jane Austen La Rochefoucauld	Descartes Pascal Hobbes Spinoza Locke Berkeley Leibniz Hume Kant	Locke Rousseau Adam Smith *U.S. Constitution* Hamilton, Madison, Jay Tocqueville	Galileo Kepler Young Euler Mayer S. Carnot L. Carnot Kelvin Taylor	D. Bernoulli Newton Leibniz Huygens Dedekind Maxwell	Mozart
Molière Goethe Tolstoy Dostoevski Baudelaire Valéry Yeats Kafka Wallace Stevens T. S. Eliot Mark Twain James Joyce	Hegel Kierkegaard Neitzsche William James Wittgenstein	Hegel Marx Documents from American Political History Tocqueville Lincoln Supreme Court Opinions Keynes	Faraday Lobachevski Lorenz Rutherford Minkowski Bernard Davisson Dreisch Boveri Weismann John Maynard Smith	de Broglie Mendel J. J. Thomson Bohr Millikan Schrödinger Darwin Freud Einstein Heisenberg Whitehead Maxwell	Wagner

NOTES

Unless otherwise indicated, all records of meetings of the faculty and of the Board of Visitors and Governors are located in the archives of St. John's College in Annapolis.

Chapter 1

1. Gerald Grant and David Riesman, *The Perpetual Dream* (Chicago: University of Chicago Press, 1979).
2. Stringfellow Barr, "Scott Buchanan, Teacher," *Center Magazine* (November 1968), published by the Center for the Study of Democratic Institutions. "It was Buchanan who conceived, established, and continuously developed the St. John's program." See also a letter from Jacob Klein to Victor Butterfield (December 22, 1954), "Scott Buchanan is the real founder of St. John's College as it is now."
3. Harris Wofford, Jr., ed., *Embers of the World,* Conversations with Scott Buchanan (Santa Barbara: Center for the Study of Democratic Institutions, 1969).
4. Barr, "Scott Buchanan, Teacher," 58.
5. "Harvard Manifesto," January 17, 1924, Buchanan Files, Houghton Library, Harvard University.
6. Scott Buchanan, *Poetry and Mathematics* (with a new introduction) (Philadelphia: Lippincott, 1962), 14.
7. Buchanan, *Poetry and Mathematics,* 19.
8. Buchanan, *Poetry and Mathematics,* 19.
9. Eva T. H. Brann, "The Program of St. John's College," *Toward the Restoration of the Liberal Arts Curriculum:* A Rockefellar Foundation Conference, September 28, 1978 (New York: The Rockefellar Foundation, 1979).
10. Jefferson to Carr, August 19, 1785, Adrienne Koch and William Peden, eds., *The Life and Selected Writings by Thomas Jefferson* (Modern Library, 1944), 375.
11. Jefferson to Benjamin Rush, January 16, 1811, *The Life and Selected Writings,* 609.
12. Resolution of the Board of Visitors of the University of Virginia, March 24, 1825.
13. Edmund S. Walsh, SJ, *Education of the Founding Fathers of the Republic* (Freeport, N.Y.: Books for Libraries Press, 1935). Walsh even claims that the education of the founding fathers was essentially the same as that received in the schools of the Middle Ages. He bases this conclusion on an examination of certain theses that were presented in colonial colleges for students to defend. Some of these theses might have indeed been maintained by scholastic philosophers, as, for example, "God is the cause of all things." But others are distinctly modern theses, as for example, the Lockean thesis "In the state of nature a man is the owner of all that he secured possession of before others." Walsh was not able to distinguish between what is medieval and what is modern.
14. Jefferson to an unnamed member of the University of Virginia faculty, October 25, 1825, in Saul Padover, *The Complete Jefferson* (Distributed by Duell, Sloan & Pierce, Inc., N.Y. 1943), 1094.

15. Jefferson to John Adams, October 13, 1813, Padover, *Complete Jefferson,* 951.
16. Mortimer J. Adler, *Philosopher at Large* (New York: Macmillan, 1977), 82ff.
17. *Embers of the World,* 15.

Chapter 2

1. Buchanan to Mortimer Adler, Buchanan Files, Houghton Library, Harvard University.
2. Buchanan to Adler, October 30, 1929, Buchanan Files.
3. Buchanan to Adler, October 30, 1929, Buchanan Files.
4. Buchanan to Adler, March 14, 1932, Adler Files, Institute for Philosophical Research, Chicago, Ill.
5. Buchanan to Adler, March 14, 1932, Adler Files.
6. Buchanan to Adler, March 14, 1932, Adler Files.
7. Buchanan to Adler, March 15, 1932, Adler Files.
8. Scott Buchanan, *Poetry and Mathematics* (with a new introduction) (Philadelphia: Lippincott, 1962), 26.
9. This goes beyond what Aristotle envisaged, since for him the life lived in the quest for philosophic wisdom does not require practical wisdom in the largest sense, and the life lived in accordance with the most comprehensive practical wisdom, i.e., the political life, does not necessarily presuppose the search for philosophic wisdom. Neither kind of life requires a wisdom that guides the hand like that of a sculptor or potter.
10. Buchanan, *Poetry and Mathematics,* 27. Buchanan, in an article entitled "A Crisis in Liberal Education" published in February 1938 in the Amherst *Graduates' Quarterly,* acknowledged that the program as proposed in the Virginia Report was intended for "the better students." By the time he became dean at St. John's he had come to think of it as a form of education suitable for all students of college age.
11. Buchanan Files.
12. Barr received the nickname, "Winkie," when a very small boy because of his fascination with a nursery rhyme that used to be repeated to him by his maternal grandfather, the Reverend Frank Stringfellow, an Episcopal priest, who, as a scout for General Robert E. Lee during the Civil War, had had many extraordinary adventures. The rhyme went:

    Hokey, pokey, winkie, wunk
    Chubberly, cummery, chummerly, chunk.
    Hangery, wangery, chingery, changery,
    King of the Cannibal Islands.

13. Buchanan Files.
14. Buchanan Files.
15. Mortimer J. Adler, *Philosopher at Large* (New York: Macmillan, 1977), 91.
16. Adler, *Philosopher at Large,* 176.
17. In one of his conversations with Harris Wofford, he says, "I'm not a good Thomist." (Harris Woford, ed., *Embers of the World,* conversations with Scott Buchanan (Santa Barbara: Center for the Study of Democratic Institutions, 1969), 15.) A year or two after McKeon went to Chicago, he returned to the Columbis campus, and at a gathering of friends, among whom was Irwin Ed-

man, remarked, "I'm troubled by the rumor that I'm a Thomist. I'm an Ockhamite." Edman replied, "What do they think about that around the Loop?" The story was told to me by Jacques Barzun, who was present at the gathering.
18. Buchanan to Adler, November 13, 1935, Adler Files.
19. Adler, *Philosopher at Large,* 176.
20. Buchanan, *Poetry and Mathematics,* 28-9.
21. Buchanan, *Poetry and Mathematics,* 29.
22. *Embers of the World,* 87. See also transcript of a taped conversation with Allan Hoffman, July 13, 1975, St. John's College Archives.
23. Transcript of a recorded conversation between Barr and Buchanan made in 1966 at the Center for the Study of Democratic Institutions.
24. St. John's Board Minutes, June 4, 1937.
25. Barr to the Board, June 19, 1937, appended to the Board Minutes for June 4, 1937.
26. Baltimore *Sun,* July 11, 1937.
27. *New York Times,* July 7, 1937.
28. In a recent account of the St. John's curriculum, Eva T. H. Brann describes a great book as one that is occupied with the perennial questions, and goes on to say that this is "the very antithesis of the claim that such questions have no answers," since that claim means that one presumes to know more than anyone can know. It may, nonetheless, be true that the most important of perennial questions have not yet received compelling answers and are, for all that, still worth pursuing, or indeed, because of their intrinsic depth, breadth, and height, more than any others worth pursuing.
29. Buchanan Files.
30. Baltimore *Sun,* August 4. 1937.
31. Transcript, Barr and Buchanan conversation, 1966.

Chapter 3
1. Charter of St. John's College, granted by the General Assembly as part of Chapter 37 of the Laws of Maryland of 1784.
2. *St. John's Collegian,* September 21, 1937.
3. St. John's Board Minutes, January 10, 1938.
4. Baltimore *Sun* January 18, 1938.
5. During the entire time that Barr and Buchanan were at St. John's, no faculty member had tenure. All were on one-year appointments.
6. Transcript of a recorded conversation between Barr and Buchanan made in 1966 at the Center for the Study of Democratic Institutions.
7. Scott Buchanan, *Possibility* (London: Kegan Paul, 1922), 111.
8. Harris Wofford, Jr., ed., *Embers of the World,* Conversations with Scott Buchanan (Santa Barbara: Center for the Study of the Democratic Institutions, 1969), 26.
9. Scott Buchanan, *Poetry and Mathematics* (with new introduction) (Philadelphia: Lippincott, 1962), 57-60.
10. Buchanan, *Poetry and Mathematics,* 89.
11. *Embers of the World,* 140.

12. Thomas Aquinas, *Summa Theologiae,* II–II, A 25, a. 12.
13. When the author came to St. John's in 1941, the books in the college library were classified under the headings of the seven liberal arts, the chemistry books under music, perhaps because of number ratios.
14. Mortimer J. Adler, *Philosopher at Large* (New York: Macmillan, 1977), 93.
15. Medea, after all, is not very much like the Virgin Mary.
16. This author's notes to lectures by Buchanan on metaphysics, given at the University of Virginia 1934–35. Buchanan gives a partial account of the transcendentals in *The Doctrine of Signatures* (London: K. Paul, Trench, Trubner & Co., 1938).
17. Report to Robert M. Hutchins, 1937, Buchanan Files, Houghton Library, Harvard University.
18. John S. Kieffer, "Memories of 1937 and After," an unpublished manuscript.
19. Transcript, Barr and Buchanan conversation, 1966.

Chapter 4

1. Walter Lippman, "Today and Tomorrow," *New York Herald Tribune,* December 27, 1938.
2. Baltimore *Evening Sun,* January 23, 24, 25, 1939.
3. *Life* magazine, February 5, 1940.
4. I Esdras 3:18ff.
5. Buchanan to Brameld, December 16, 1938, St. John's College Archives.
6. *St. John's Collegian,* November 18, 1938, 1.
7. *St. John's Collegian,* February 29, 1939, editorial, 2.
8. St. John's Faculty Minutes, November 16, 1940.
9. Buchanan to Miller, July 14, 1937, St. John's College Archives.
10. St. John's Board Minutes, August 16, 1937.
11. Stringfellow Barr, Informal Lecture to Summer Freshmen on the History of the St. John's Program, July 28, 1972, St. John's College Archives.
12. Buchanan to Miller, July 14, 1937.
13. Barr to Hutchins, September 26, 1938, St. John's College Archives.
14. Barr to Adler, October 25, 1938, St. John's College Archives.

Chapter 5

1. John Dewey, "Challenge to Liberal Thought," *Fortune,* August 1944.
2. Alexander Meiklejohn, "A Reply to John Dewey," *Fortune,* January 1945.
3. John Dewey, Letter to the Editors, *Fortune,* March 1945.
4. Sidney Hook, *Education for Modern Man* (New York: Dial Press, 1946), 209.
5. Hook, *Education,* 21, 213.
6. Buchanan to Hook, November 10, 1938, St. John's College Archives.
7. Buchanan to Hook, December 15, 1942, St. John's College Archives.
8. Hook to Buchanan, January 26, 1943, St. John's College Archives.
9. Buchanan to Emily S. Hamblen, April 27, 1940, St. John's College Archives.
10. *Nineteen Forty Yearbook,* 15.
11. *St. John's Collegian,* October 27, 1939, 1.
12. *Nineteen Forty-two Yearbook,* 14.
13. *Nineteen Forty-two Yearbook,* 25.

14. *Nineteen Forty-three Yearbook,* 20.
15. Robert Hutchins thought this a good idea anyway, believing that the last two years of high school were usually wasted.
16. *Nineteen Forty-two Yearbook,* 7.
17. *Nineteen Forty-four Yearbook,* 8.
18. *Nineteen Forty-five — Forty-six Yearbook,* 11.
19. Buchanan to H. G. Cayley, August 25, 1937, St. John's College Archives.
20. *Nineteen Forty-five — Forty-six Yearbook,* 13.

Chapter 6

1. In 1868 the Naval Academy had purchased from St. John's a triangular piece of land of which a part of King George Street is one side.
2. St. John's Faculty Minutes, September 1940.
3. St. John's Board Minutes, January 31, 1941.
4. Buchanan Files, Houghton Library, Harvard University.
5. Board Minutes, February 25, 1945.
6. Diary of James V. Forrestal, copy in the Navy Operational Archives, Naval Historical Center, Washington, D.C.
7. Record of the hearing before the Committee on Naval Affairs of the U. S. Senate (June 20, 1945), Navy Library, Washington, D.C. Cf. the testimony of Captain T. R. Wirth, representing the Superintendent of the Academy, at the same hearing.
8. Copies of letters in the Buchanan Files.
9. Buchanan to Hutchins, May 7, 1945, Buchanan Files.
10. Hutchins to Buchanan, May 9, 1945, Buchanan Files.
11. Buchanan to Senator Wayne Morse, undated, Buchanan Files.
12. Baltimore *Sun,* April 1945.
13. Baltimore *Sun,* July 3, 1945; *Washington Post,* July 30, 1945.
14. Dean's Nine Year Report (1946), St. John's College Archives.
15. Cf. the Supreme Court decision in Kohl v. United States (1875).
16. *Evening Capital,* October 22, 1945.
17. Testimony before the House Naval Affairs Committee, October 9, 1945.
18. Statement of Richard Cleveland before the Senate Naval Affairs Committee, June, 20, 1945.
19. Captain T. R. Wirth indeed stated at the Senate Committee hearing of June 20, "Acquisition of the St. John's property is urgently required in the national interest to provide the area determined to be essential to the continuance of the Naval Academy mission: the fundamental education and training of the number of young men required for the commissioned officer personnel of the United States Navy." This, of course, was not an official declaration of policy by the Navy Department or the Committees.
20. Diary of James V. Forrestal.
21. Minutes of the Board meetings for 1944–47 are missing.
22. Buchanan Files.
23. *Evening Capital,* August 1, 1945.
24. Memorandum by Richard Cleveland to the St. John's College Board, St. John's College Archives.
25. Statement of Policy by the Board of Visitors and Governors of St. John's Col-

lege, with reference to the Navy Department's proposal to acquire the St. John's campus (November 21, 1945), St. John's College Archives.
26. Buchanan had discovered from studying the Dartmouth case that the charter of a college confers upon it immortality.
27. Dean's Report, *St. John's Collegian,* October 19, 1945.
28. Statement of Policy, November 21, 1945.
29. Mellon to Barr, appended to the St. John's Faculty Minutes for April 27, 1946.
30. Transcript of a recorded conversation with Allan Hoffman, July 13, 1975: "I thought, why not put an end to it by putting the college where the huge beast couldn't suddenly attack it again? And it was clear that a lot of people in the Navy were damned determined to attack again." St. John's College Archives. Since 1946 there has been no attempt by the Navy to take the campus.
31. Hoffman conversation.
32. Hoffman conversation.
33. Memorandum to the Board of Visitors and Governors, July 31, 1946, St. John's College Archives.
34. Announcement by the Board of St. John's College, August 3, 1946, Buchanan Files.
35. Buchanan to Adler, August 14, 1946, Adler Files, Institute for Philosophical Research, Chicago.
36. Faculty Minutes, November 2, 1946.
37. Buchanan to Cleveland, November 20, 1946, Buchanan Files.
38. Buchanan to Hutchins, December 5, 1946, Buchanan Files.
39. Mellon to Barr, June 24, 1947, Buchanan Files.
40. Hoffman conversation.
41. Faculty Minutes, September 15, 1947.
42. Buchanan to Kieffer, June 8, 1948, St. John's College Archives.
43. Hoffman conversation.

Chapter 7

1. Buchanan to Cleveland, January 15, 1947, Buchanan Files, Houghton Library, Harvard University.
2. Cleveland to Buchanan, Buchanan Files.
3. St. John's Faculty Minutes, January 8, 1948.
4. *Nineteen Forty-eight Yearbook,* 11.
5. Faculty Minutes, April 17, 1948.
6. St. John's Board Minutes, January 30, 1949.
7. Board Minutes, September 17, 1949.

Chapter 8

1. St. John's *Collegian,* January 1949.
2. Jacob Klein and Leo Strauss, "A Giving of Accounts," *The College,* April 1970.
3. Klein and Strauss, "Giving."
4. Toeplitz to Professor K. Loewner, September 5, 1934.
5. Klein to Else Tammann Husserl, October 18, 1938.
6. *Bulletin of St. John's College:* Statement of Educational Policy and Program, December 1952.

7. *Bulletin of St. John's College,* November 1968.
8. *The St. John's Program,* A Report (Annapolis: St. John's College Press, 1955).

Chapter 9

1. St. John's Board Minutes, February 15, 1958.
2. Board Minutes, October 1, 1960.
3. Board Minutes, May 21, 1949.
4. Board Minutes, April 15, 1950.
5. Board Minutes, September 16, 1950.
6. Board Minutes, October 1, 1955.
7. Board Minutes, December 15, 1956.
8. Two of the committee, Clarence J. Kramer and Thomas Simpson, later became members of the St. John's faculty. Rogers Albritton became a professor of philosophy at Harvard. John Mack went on to a distinguished career in business, William Ross entered the practice of law and was, at one time, chairman of the administrative law section of the American Bar Association. The chairman, Vernon Derr, is now Deputy Director of the Wave Propogation Laboratory of the National Oceanic and Atmospheric Administration in Boulder, Colorado.
9. *Catalogue of St. John's College,* 1938-39.
10. Report of the Student Laboratory Committee, 1948, St. John's College Archives.
11. Board Minutes, December 6, 1952.
12. *The St. John's Program,* A Report (Annapolis: St. John's College Press, 1955).
13. *Bulletin of St. John's College:* Statement of Educational Policy and Program, 1951.
14. *St. John's Program,* 1955.
15. Chapter 8.
16. Jacob Klein: Lecture entitled "Speech, Its Strength and Its Weaknesses," St. John's College Library.
17. *Bulletin of St. John's College,* Report of the President, January 1959.
18. Board Minutes, February 5, 1958.
19. Board Minutes, February 5, 1958.